# RETURN OF THE STRONG GODS

# RETURN
## OF THE
# STRONG
# GODS

*Nationalism, Populism, and
the Future of the West*

# R. R. RENO

REGNERY GATEWAY
Washington, D.C.

Regnery Gateway™ is a trademark of Salem Communications Holding Corporation Regnery® is a registered trademark and its colophon is a trademark of Salem Communications Holding Corporation

Cataloging-in-Publication data on file with the Library of Congress

First trade paperback edition published 2021

ISBN 978-1-68451-269-0

Published in the United States by
Regnery Gateway, an imprint of
Regnery Publishing
A Division of Salem Media Group
Washington, D.C.
www.Regnery.com

Manufactured in the United States of America

10 9 8 7 6 5 4 3 2 1

Books are available in quantity for promotional or premium use. For information on discounts and terms, please visit our website: www.Regnery.com.

# CONTENTS

Preface      ix

Introduction      xix

CHAPTER ONE
**The Postwar Consensus**      1

CHAPTER TWO
**Therapies of Disenchantment**      33

CHAPTER THREE
**Weakening as Destiny**      71

CHAPTER FOUR
**The Homeless Society**      97

CHAPTER FIVE
**The Return of the Strong Gods**      135

Afterword      163

Acknowledgements      167
Notes      169
Index      175

# Preface

A few months after this book was published, the strong gods returned.

Panic struck in March 2020 as a virus originating in China spread around the world. Fear of death and disease rippled through the population, especially among influential, university-educated people, who in the West are especially anxious about their health and safety. Politicians responded by throwing entire countries into lockdown, an unprecedented measure that put society in a state of suspended animation for months.

Nature abhors a vacuum—especially human nature, which is sociable and restless. In June 2020, amid the existential void of the universal lockdown, police in Minneapolis arrested an agitated, unruly black man named George Floyd, who died under restraint. The result was an explosion of protests across the United States that often descended into violence and looting.

We can argue endlessly about what killed George Floyd—drugs in his bloodstream, vicious police tactics, a criminal justice system that targets blacks. We can speculate why protests spread so quickly—systemic racism, endemic violence in poor black communities, networks of professional agitators. But one thing is indisputable: In the vacuum of lockdown, blood cried out from the ground. After a long season of turmoil and confinement, the rhetoric of diversity and inclusion seemed ineffectual. It was replaced by strident demands for retribution, reparation, and punishment. "No justice, no peace." This is the slogan of a strong god.

We should not judge movements by extreme voices, but anyone who wishes to understand the events inspired by the slogan "Black Lives Matter" must pay attention to what people say, especially people of influence. In early June 2021, a woman named Aruna Khilanani revealed her "fantasies of unloading a revolver into the head of any White person that got in my way, burying their body and wiping my bloody hands as I walked away relatively guiltless with a bounce in my step." Khilanani is not an anger-addled street-corner crank but a psychiatrist, and her words, uttered in a lecture at the Yale School of Medicine, expressed more than political correctness. She was there to worship the strong god of vengeance.

In the ensuing controversy, Khilanani insisted that she had been exaggerating for rhetorical effect, which was no doubt true. But how and when we exaggerate is revealing. Impatient with calm discussion and meticulous analysis, she will no longer deliberate about "root causes." Her remarks excluded all softening gestures such as "sharing perspectives" or "hearing new voices." The hot hyperbole rejected the open-society slogans that have dominated for so long, clichés that soften civic life and make things more porous and fluid, formulations that weaken strong claims and blur sharp boundaries.

Khilanani's talk of guns and blood points in a very different direction. A powerful consensus in favor of fluid openness was embraced by the left and right in recent decades. I call it the postwar consensus, because I trace its origins to the American-led reconstruction of the West after Auschwitz. In my reading of recent history, that fell name denotes more than a death camp in Poland. It sums up the entire orgy of destruction that began in the trenches of World War I and ended with mushroom clouds over Hiroshima and Nagasaki. The consensus that took hold after 1945 sought to dissolve the political passions that many deemed to be the underlying cause of those decades of violence. The postwar consensus sought to banish the strong gods.

By the first decade of the twenty-first century, the postwar consensus supported a power-sharing arrangement between the Democratic Party, favoring go-fast liquefaction of traditional culture and go-slow economic deregulation, and the Republican Party, favoring go-fast economic deregulation with the hope of not-too-fast cultural deregulation. When I wrote *Return of the Strong Gods*, the establishment consensus in favor of openness was plain to see. And when I was writing, a rejection of open borders, open trade, and other fruits of the postwar consensus by the populist right was also obvious. The events of 2020 indicate that the strong gods are returning on the American left as well.

The book you have in your hands offers a succinct history of the past seven decades, most of which I have experienced as a teenager and adult. I distrust the sufficiency of singular explanations, including my own. Technological innovations (the Pill, for example) shaped that history, as did international events and economic developments. There exists no Lord of the Rings in social analysis, no single explanation that rules them all.

But I remain confident in the basic story I tell. After 1945, our ruling class agreed that powerful loves and intense loyalties make us easily manipulated by demagogues. Our passions hurl us into disastrous conflicts and brutal ideological movements. Our only hope, the postwar consensus holds, is to tamp down our loves and loyalties, to weaken them with skepticism, nonjudgmentalism, and a political commitment to an open society.

And I argue that the wheel of history is turning. The gods of weakening are losing their power over public life. Donald Trump horrified the establishment because he derided the open-society consensus. His brash Americanism, his promises to tear up trade deals, and his loud talk of building a wall thrilled voters who wanted reconsolidation not deregulation, protection not limitless openness.

You can find Trump odious or inspiring. You can reject or affirm his political priorities. But a sober observer recognizes that Trump rose to prominence because an angry populace felt betrayed by the postwar consensus. What I did not see while writing this book is that the American left, which opposed Trump bitterly, would pivot to affirm the return of its own strong gods.

Only yesterday, multicultural managers and HR bureaucrats spoke solemnly of diversity and inclusion, vague notions that serve the gods of weakening. Today, however, the same managers and bureaucrats add "equity," a term that signifies a change in direction. Equity operates in the domain of justice, and justice promises not "diversity" but the right result. Equity encourages strong measures— condemning the unjust, punishing the oppressors, denouncing the unfairly advantaged and the wrongly privileged. Diversity is a feel-good word. Equity topples statues.

I cannot pretend to know the future. I can only take the measure of present trends. The postwar consensus trusted that a better future could be achieved by removing barriers, setting aside traditional mores, empowering individual choice, and letting markets decide. The sudden prominence of the rhetoric of equity suggests that many on the left are losing confidence in the promise of an open society. They now demand racial and sexual quotas, hard numerical measurements that cannot be evaded with avowals of good intentions. As the right demands clear and enforced borders, the left demands clear and enforced results. It wants a just society (as it conceives of it), not an open society. And it is willing to rule with an iron fist to achieve that goal.

I am suspicious of those who turn too quickly to Nazi Germany for analogies that illuminate our present distempers. But if we remain sober and do not allow ourselves to be swept up into moral and political panic, we can detect parallels. In the 1920s, conservatives in Germany distrusted the procedural justice and commercial ethos of the Weimar Republic, believing that a good society would not automatically evolve in accord with liberal principles and market forces. The future, they argued, must be shaped by a decisive act of will. A similar view is emerging on the left. Progressives are impatient. Free speech? Merit? Procedural justice? Laws prohibiting discrimination on the basis of race? These formal commitments must be set aside, we are told, because they stand in the way of transformative justice.

And so it is not only Trump and the populist right that wants the strong gods to return. Many on the American left look to blood for answers, a vengeful and punitive image that suggests strong gods with grim designs. They champion blood's binding power, its demand for justice, and its powerful symbolism of moral and political urgency. The signs of the times suggest that the historical thesis of this book is correct. The postwar era is ending. The strong gods are returning. Let us work to ensure that they are ennobling, not debasing, that they rebuild and renew rather than tear down and degrade.

*Return of the Strong Gods* has been criticized from a number of angles. I will not try to respond to all of them, but it is useful to consider some. Some have complained that my talk of "strong gods" is imprecise and obscure. Yes, but every consequential episode in human history is blurry and opaque, including the past seventy years. My aim is to illuminate, as best I can, our political and cultural struggles, which have become intense. The metaphor of "strong gods" casts useful light on our situation.

Friends counsel that I should be less enthusiastic about the return of the strong gods. I am fully aware of the dangers they pose, which is why, following the Bible, I urge a politics of noble loves. The Book of Wisdom begins with an extended allegory. Lady Wisdom goes through the city, explaining to men the bad consequences of their liaisons with prostitutes and loose women (a metaphor for idolatry). But the men are smitten, and the arguments of Lady Wisdom have no effect. Returning to her palace, she prepares a great banquet and sends her beautiful young attendants into the public square to draw in the men of the city. They come to feast, and their perverse loves are corrected by the higher love of Lady Wisdom. The open society tries to buy peace with dispassion and small ambitions, encouraging critique and other techniques of weakening. This approach will not succeed in the long run. The only reliable safeguards against debased political passions are elevated ones.

Though many defend the status quo, I will not raise my voice in defense of the dying postwar consensus. In this book, I argue that the West overreacted. Intent on countering the evils of Auschwitz and all it represented, we embarked on a utopian project of living without shared loves and strong loyalties. Human nature was never going to allow that project to succeed. We are made for love, not open-ended diversity, limitless inclusion, and relentless critique. The postwar consensus went too far, emptying our souls and desiccating our societies. So yes, the strong gods can be dangerous. But they make transcendence possible. They restore to public life spiritual drama and shared purpose.

Christian allies warn that I am insufficiently alive to the danger that populism will make an idol of the nation. In Plato's *Symposium*, Socrates recounts the teaching of Diotima, his mentor, who observed that we often love finite goods as if they were ultimate. But this is not reason to despair. For once aroused, love's ardor can be directed toward a ladder that rises from lower loves to higher ones. I hold the Platonic view. There is no guarantee that we will climb the ladder of love. Misjudging lesser goods as the highest good (the essence of idolatry) always remains a danger. But the unstated premise behind this book is that life without love is a greater evil than life in which finite loves are made absolute. I have argued for this premise in other works (see especially the essays in *Fighting the Noonday Devil*). Put simply, to love wrongly is dangerous, but however debasing, it is human. By contrast, to fail to love is inhuman. The deepest failure of the postwar consensus, then, is that it trains us to be loveless and therefore to be something less than human.

Let me issue my own theological warning: Beware iconoclasm. It is a heresy born of the fantasy that we can eliminate the possibility of idolatry by destroying every object of love other than the highest, which is God. Thomas Aquinas taught that grace perfects nature; it does not destroy nature. Family, team, city, country—these social spheres rightly win our love and command our loyalty. We can be seduced and blinded by our loves. A great deal can go wrong, which is why Jesus warns us that our love of God may require us to hate our father. The same holds for fatherland. But our capacity for perversion does not destroy these natural goods. They remain worthy of our love if we will but love rightly.

Liberal allies worry that I court a dangerous illiberalism. Their concerns are overwrought, but they have a basis in truth. Our liberal traditions aim to limit the role of religious and metaphysical passions in public life. In this regard, liberalism harkens to the gods of weakening. The open-society consensus gained traction after 1945 so easily because it drew upon the liberalism that is an important part of our Anglo-American inheritance. Like my liberal critics, I cherish this inheritance. Let us by all means defend the Bill of Rights and other honorable components of our liberal tradition. But let us also remember that liberalism tempers and moderates; it does not initiate. It weeds the field but does not plant. When liberalism becomes dominant, as it has done in the postwar consensus, civic life withers, for liberalism offers no vigorous language of love.

For everything there is a season. In this book I argue that our historical moment begs for the restoration of shared loves. We must not fail to meet this need. In my estimation, only an uplifting politics of solidarity can counter identity politics, which makes a dark promise of solidarity, one based on blood, chromosomes, and sexual appetites. In this historical moment, full of the confusion and danger that attend the collapse of a governing consensus, we need something more than liberalism. We need strong gods, purified by reason and subordinate to true religion but nevertheless powerful enough to win our hearts. I have cryptically thanked Philip Rieff in my acknowledgements. I never met him, but as a young theological scholar I read his books. A brilliant sociologist, he despaired of the desacralization promoted by so-called critical reason, which he believed was leading us to an anti-culture, a "third world" of spiritual impoverishment heretofore unknown to men. And Rieff despaired over his despair. In his agony of unbelief, he pointed me toward a fundamental truth: it is more precious to love than to know.

Of course, the Bible says as much. Love of God is the first commandment, and as the First Letter of John teaches, "Love is of God, and he who loves is born of God and knows God." As I have already noted, Plato strikes a similar note. I should not have needed Philip Rieff to guide me to such an obvious truth. But I did need him. He reasoned his way to the dark bottom of the postwar consensus, allowing me to see that the opposite of love is not hate but death, the placid cessation of aspiration and desire, the tempting void of nothingness.

The spasms of violence in the twentieth century rose to great heights, casting a long shadow over our moral and political ideals and even over our spiritual imaginations, as I show in this book. The postwar consensus was originally modest. I would have supported the efforts of men like James B. Conant, and in fact I did in my younger days. But as it developed and became more and more rigid in its dogmatic openness, that consensus became an enemy of love.

I am more than sixty years old. The only society I have known is the one dominated by the postwar consensus. I am therefore a largely blind guide to whatever comes next. But of this I am sure: it will require a restoration of love. And love is roused by the strong gods, which is why they are returning.

# Introduction

A young friend in Australia sent me an essay that read like a flaming indictment of the status quo. It ended with the arresting sentence, "I am twenty-seven years old and hope to live to see the end of the twentieth century." That sounds paradoxical, but it isn't. The rhythms of history do not always align with the calendar. Historians refer to the "long nineteenth century." It began in 1789 with the French Revolution and ended in 1914 with the slaughter of World War I. We seem to be reaching another turning point. The violence that traumatized the West between 1914 and 1945 evoked a powerful, American-led response that was anti-fascist, anti-totalitarian, anti-colonialist, anti-imperialist, and anti-racist. These *anti* imperatives define the postwar era. Their aim is to dissolve the strong beliefs and powerful loyalties thought to have fueled the conflicts that convulsed the twentieth century.

When communism crumbled, many announced the inauguration of a new era. Some spoke of the "short twentieth century," which ran from 1914 to 1991. But as my young correspondent recognizes, the fall of the Soviet Union did not bring the postwar era to a close, for it marked not the end of the *anti* imperatives but rather their intensification. During the past few decades, anti-fascism, anti-racism, anti-colonialism, and the rest have been pursued with unstinting fervor. After 1989, we did not relax our vigilance. On the contrary, people began to monitor pronouns and search for "microaggressions" to punish.

These manifestations of political correctness are not epiphenomenal. They are late fruits of a singular historical judgment. In the second half of the twentieth century, we came to regard the first half as a world-historical eruption of the evils inherent in the Western tradition, which can be corrected only by the relentless pursuit of openness, disenchantment, and weakening. That pursuit was already implicit in liberalism, as Alasdair MacIntyre, Patrick Deneen, and others have pointed out. But after 1945 it became paramount, with nuance at first, but over time with greater ideological rigidity. The *anti* imperatives are now flesh-eating dogmas masquerading as the fulfillment of the anti-dogmatic spirit. So my young friend is trapped. The recent, undying century won't pass from the scene. Its *anti* imperatives have become sleepless monitors of public life, depriving him of solidarity born of shared loves and loyalties, the solidarity any normal human being seeks.

The death grip of the *anti* imperatives on the West is plain to see. After Donald Trump's election, a number of mainstream journalists collapsed in hysterics: He was an "authoritarian" of one sort or another. The same goes for European populism. A specter is haunting Europe, countless journalists and opinion writers warn—the specter of fascism. Tract after tract has likened our times to Germany during the 1930s. Indeed, it is a sign of nuance when a member of our chattering class compares Trump to the Spanish strongman Francisco Franco rather than to Hitler. Today's intelligentsia compulsively return to the trying decades of the early twentieth century. It is as if they desperately want to keep the last century going, insisting that the fight against fascism remains our fight.

This is absurd. It is not 1939. Our societies are not gathering themselves into masses marching in lockstep. Central planners do not clog our economies. There is no longer an overbearing bourgeois culture bent on "exclusion." Bull Connor isn't commissioner of public safety in Birmingham. Instead, our societies are dissolving. Economic globalization shreds the social contract. Identity politics disintegrates civic bonds. A uniquely Western anti-Western multiculturalism deprives people of their cultural inheritance. Mass migration reshapes the social landscape. Courtship, marriage, and family no longer form our moral imaginations. Borders are porous, even the one that separates men from women. Tens of thousands die of heroin overdoses. Hundreds of thousands are aborted. Of course my young friend wants the twentieth century to end. So do I.

I am not opposed to the anti-totalitarian struggles of the last century. The postwar consensus arose for good reasons. Social convulsions and mass mobilizations dominated the lives of those born in the late nineteenth and early twentieth centuries. World War I mustered millions of young men into armies of unprecedented size and marched them into inconclusive battles producing casualties on a shocking scale. No European country emerged from the conflict unchanged.

The armistice of November 1918 did not produce a lasting peace. Mussolini, proclaiming a "revolutionary nationalism," led his paramilitary troops into Rome in 1922 and assumed unchecked power. The Bolsheviks consolidated their grip on Russia and purged their adversaries. The Weimar Republic, established in Germany after World War I, became a byword for decadence and ineffectual governance. Spain exploded in a civil war that foreshadowed what many feared was the inevitable conflict between two forms of revolutionary modernism, one ordered to a communist utopia and the other promising to renew society through racial purity and national power. The streets rang with declarations: the Dictatorship of the Proletariat, the Triumph of the Will, Blood and Soil. In those years, fierce gods trampled the benign managerial habits of commerce and the liberal norms of free consent and democratic deliberation. Strong and dark gods stormed through Europe, eventually setting aflame most of the world and bringing death to millions.

It is difficult to grasp the ruin facing the West after World War II. My grandfather was a field artillery officer, a member of the Army Reserve activated after Pearl Harbor. Sent to Europe after the invasion of Normandy, he crossed the Rhine with the Third Army in late March 1945. For the next forty days they raced across southern Germany, his unit towing eight-inch howitzers day and night, unlimbering their guns for only an hour here or there to destroy what remained of the German armies. In his wartime photograph album is a picture of the cathedral in Munich, strangely preserved amidst a scene of extensive destruction. Not a soul was to be seen in the empty, devastated streets.

His album also contained pictures of mass graves and the skeletal, barely living survivors of a liberated concentration camp. As a child I asked him if he had taken the pictures. "No, I was sick that day and gave my camera to another officer." At the time, I took his reply at face value. Later, I recognized that he was in all likelihood telling the truth about being sick but not about who took the pictures.

My grandfather participated in the collective gasp of horror: the flattened cities, the countless dead, the wreckage of societies ravaged by war, and cruelty that bled into insanity. The conservative critic Richard Weaver wrote to a friend after Japan capitulated in August 1945, "Is anything saved? We cannot be sure. True, there are a few buildings left standing around, but what kind of animal is going to inhabit them?"[1] The scale of destruction was deeply traumatizing. Even nature herself was violated in orgies of bombardment. A few years after the war's end, Albert Camus, with poetic irony, twisted the Nazi image of solidarity rooted in blood and soil into an aching lament: "Disaster is today our common fatherland."

In Germany, they speak of the demise of the Nazi regime on May 8, 1945, as *Stunde Null*, zero hour. The sense of hitting bottom was widely shared, even among the victors. The years from 1914 through 1945 were dark with calamity. As I hope to show in these pages, almost all our intuitions about how to promote justice and serve the common good have been formed by this civilizational *shoah*.

We continue to define ourselves culturally, even spiritually, as anti-totalitarian, anti-fascist, anti-racist, and anti-nationalist. I call the atmosphere of opinion that sustains these *anti* imperatives the "postwar consensus." Although there has been political contention between the left and the right, it has been a sibling rivalry. As I will show, the postwar left fixed its attention on moral freedom and cultural deregulation, seeing them as natural extensions of the anti-authoritarian imperative, while the postwar right focused on economic freedom and market deregulation for similar anti-totalitarian reasons. As the long twentieth century ends, this unified thrust is easier to discern, not least because the establishment left and right are closing ranks to denounce populism.

The postwar consensus is more than political. Its powerful cultural influence is evident in the emphasis on openness and weakening in highly theorized literary criticism and cultural studies in universities, often under the flag of critique and deconstruction, and in popular calls for diversity, multiculturalism, and inclusivity, all of which entail a weakening of boundaries and opening of borders. Nor is the cultural influence of the postwar consensus confined to the left. The same insistence on openness and weakening is found in libertarianism as well, which seeks cultural deregulation so that individuals are not constrained by shared norms. It is felt in free-market economic theory and sociobiological analysis of politics and culture, both of which adopt a reductive view of human motivation that disenchants public life. Openness, weakening, and disenchantment are at play in postwar sociology, psychology, and even theology. In every instance, they rise to prominence because they are seen as necessary to prevent the return of the strong gods.

By "strong gods," I do not mean Thor and the other residents of the Old Norse Valhalla. The strong gods are the objects of men's love and devotion, the sources of the passions and loyalties that unite societies. They can be timeless. Truth is a strong god that beckons us to the matrimony of assent. They can be traditional. King and country, insofar as they still arouse men's patriotic ardor, are strong gods. The strong gods can take the forms of modern ideologies and charismatic leaders. The strong gods can be beneficent. Our constitutional piety treats the American Founding as a strong god worthy of our devotion. And they can be destructive. In the twentieth century, militarism, fascism, communism, racism, and anti-Semitism brought ruin.

Distorting the healthy intuition that the economy, politics, and culture should be ordered to the common good, fascism stokes a fevered desire for unanimity that cannot tolerate dissent. Communism turns the desire for justice into a rigid, brutal ideology. Racism and anti-Semitism express communal fears that become punitive and murderous. I take it for granted that these strong gods must be resisted. But I do not speak against them in this book. This will disturb some. We are so thoroughly trained by the *anti* imperatives of the postwar era that we often regard any failure to denounce fascism, communism, or racism as a dereliction of the duty to defend the West against its own perversions. My interest lies elsewhere. I want to understand how the West was reconstructed after 1945 in accord with openness and weakening and how they debilitate us today, threatening to destroy the Western tradition they are meant to redeem.

In the pages to follow, I will show how anti-fascism and anti-totalitarianism inspired a general theory of society. That theory has many forms, some explicit, others tacit. But it is characterized by a fundamental judgment: whatever is strong—strong loves and strong truths—leads to oppression, while liberty and prosperity require the reign of weak loves and weak truths. In the shadow of Auschwitz, this general theory has encouraged the development of a variety of anti-metaphysical philosophies and critical therapies. They are familiar to us today. When someone prefaces his remarks, "Speaking from a white, male, first-world perspective," he is warding off politically correct attacks with a gesture of piety to the weak gods. The same pattern of weakening characterizes the dictatorship of relativism, reduction to sociobiology and economic analysis, and globalist ideologies. In the first three chapters, I outline the general theory of society that took hold after 1945.

But I must be clear: This book does not offer a detailed history of the postwar era. It is an essay in the politics of the imagination. As Richard Weaver wrote in the first sentence of the first chapter of his postwar cri de coeur, *Ideas Have Consequences*, "Every man participating in a culture has three levels of conscious reflection: his specific ideas of things, his general beliefs or convictions, and his metaphysical dream of the world."[2] I contend that the postwar era saw a shift in our metaphysical dreams to openness and a lightness of being in response to the decades of catastrophe in the first half of the twentieth century.

In pursuit of those dreams the postwar imagination seeks the ministry of weak gods, or better, the gods of weakening who open things up. Today, one of our leading imperatives is inclusion, a god who softens differences. Transgression is prized for breaking down boundaries—opening things up. Diversity and multiculturalism suggest no authoritative center. The free market promises spontaneous order, miraculously coordinating our free choices, also without an authoritative center. Denigrating populist challenges to the political establishment as spasms of a "tribal mind" is a reductive critique that disenchants. I shall spell out these patterns of weakening. Rather than provide a comprehensive account, I instead analyze a few mainstream postwar figures and their important publications to illustrate influential dreamscapes, as it were. In this way I hope to illuminate the basic contrasts that have dominated the West since 1945—open versus closed, spontaneous versus authoritative, weak versus strong. The political and moral prestige of the open, spontaneous, and weak sides of these contrasts has, oddly enough, grown stronger, even authoritarian, in recent decades. Our task is to overcome this paradoxically totalitarian culture of openness and weakening.

It may be counterintuitive to describe the postwar consensus as one of openness and weakening. Political correctness is closed, hard, and punitive. But we need to distinguish the sociological reality of the dominant consensus—which is by definition bent on domination—from its content. Yes, the postwar consensus polices opinion, sometimes with an iron fist. But it does so to enforce what it imagines is best, on the whole, for society: dissolution, disintegration, and deconsolidation—in a word, openness. We're told we need more diversity, more flexibility, more innovation, more creativity, and more "difference." To speak otherwise is to risk putting oneself at odds with dominant opinion, which is always a dangerous place to stand. So yes, political correctness is in a certain sense "strong," but its punitive power is deployed to impose openness and weakening.

We must stop acting as if it were 1945. My young friend is right. The postwar consensus, however fitting in its earlier stages, is decadent. It is high time that we recognize our intellectual, moral, and spiritual freedom from the traumas that so affected our grandparents, great-grandparents, and great-great-grandparents. We need to face the challenges of the twenty-first century, not the twentieth.

This will not be easy. Today, the greatest threat to the political health of the West is not fascism or a resurgent Ku Klux Klan but a decline in solidarity and the breakdown of the trust between leaders and the led. Fearful of strong loves and committed to ever-greater openness, the postwar consensus cannot formulate, much less address, these problems. Unable to identify our shared loves—unable even to formulate the "we" that is the political subject in public life—we cannot identify the common good, the *res* in the *res publica*. Under these circumstances, increasingly prevalent in the West, civic life disintegrates into the struggle among private interests, and in this struggle the rich and powerful win. In the twenty-first century, oligarchy and an unaccountable elite pose a far greater threat to the future of liberal democracy than does the return of Hitler.

Solidarity is a ministry of the strong gods; the "we" is their gift. But the members of our leadership class cannot recognize the crisis of solidarity that threatens the West and fuels populism. They compulsively refocus attention on the problems the postwar consensus was constructed to fight: fascism, racism, conformism, and the authoritarian personality. Mention the erosion of the middle class, and someone is sure to observe that concerns about renewing solidarity amount to dangerous nostalgia. "The 1950s was an era of white male solidarity," she'll say. Someone else will object, "How can you say that lack of solidarity is our greatest problem when transgender people are still marginalized?" And if your interlocutor went to a fancy-pants university, you're likely to be chided for being "logocentric," "heteronormative," or afraid of difference.

That's if you're lucky. In all likelihood, the dominant response will be outrage, hurt, and denunciation. Professional assassination will

follow. The Southern Poverty Law Center will call you and your affil-
iates a hate group. Pressure will be applied to cut off your funding.
Diversity and inclusion must be defended!

Perhaps I'm overreacting, responding to the anti-fascist and anti-
racist hysteria of the present moment with my own hysteria. One
reason I wrote this book was to stem that tendency within myself.
We need to understand and overcome the powerful orthodoxies that
govern public life in the West—the "open-mindedness" that polices
dissent, the "diversity" in which all think alike—rather than rage
blindly against them. Hitler and the Ku Klux Klan are curses we have
inherited, a sin of the fathers visited upon their sons unto the third
and fourth generations. For those who lived in the first half of the
twentieth century, the struggle against these evils was real. Nearly a
century on, defeating them has become a destructive preoccupation.
The Manichean tendency of the postwar consensus, which insists
that either it must dominate or fascism and racism will return, blinds
our leadership class to the realities of the twenty-first century and
poisons our politics with an all-or-nothing moralism that is as self-
serving as it is destructive. These days, the rhetoric of anti-fascism,
and even that of anti-racism, has become a cynical way to discredit
those who challenge the supremacy of our elites.

Donald Trump, Viktor Orbán, and other populist challengers are
not choirboys or immaculate liberals. But their limitations are not nearly
as dangerous to the West as the fanaticism of our leadership class, whose
hyper-moralistic sense of mission—*either us or Hitler!*—prevents us from
addressing our economic, demographic, cultural, and political problems.
The growth of these problems stokes further discontent and greater
polarization, to which our leadership class responds with an amplified
anti-fascist or anti-racist rhetoric. Convinced that only they can save
the West and beholden to the postwar consensus, the rich and powerful,
not populist voters, will shipwreck our nations.

I recently picked up the *Financial Times*. I don't regularly look at that paper nowadays, though there was a time, ten or so years ago, when I subscribed, finding the editorial page the reliable but unscripted voice of neoliberal realism. Reading it now, I was reminded why I never bother to pick it up anymore. The regular writers whom I once read with interest now seem irrelevant. Some write about Donald Trump with all the bluster of the *New Yorker*, as if just *one more* column pointing out his ignorance, corruption, and evil will finally exorcise him from public life. Others interpret the populist uprisings as an epidemic of "derangement." They are not engaging the present so much as waiting for the nightmare to end. Well into the Trump administration, one *Financial Times* writer attributes Trump's victory to his ability to arouse ugly passions in "a base of angry, often elderly, white men."[3]

It seems there can be no political debate about the ways globalization has dramatically transformed the national economies of the West. Nor can these writers imagine that we must decide whether to trust the utopian promises of multicultural ideologies: that diversity will be our strength, for example, or that breaking down walls will promote harmony.

The mentality I encountered in that issue of the *Financial Times*—horror and disbelief rather than analysis and reflection—is widespread. The power of the postwar consensus makes it nearly impossible for educated people to accept its contingency—and its superannuation. Our leaders are profoundly loyal to the twentieth century, which is why my young friend's plea for permission to live in the twenty-first is achingly urgent.

The West is careening toward crisis not because of a defect deep within modernity. Our troubles do not stem from William of Ockham, the Reformation, John Locke, capitalism, or modern science and technology. It is true that there are atomizing, deracinating, deconsolidating trends in modernity. Many historians, philosophers, and social critics have pointed them out. But it is always so. The fall of man left every civilization, every era under the law of entropy, which is why renewing shared loves and unifying loyalties is one of the primary arts of leadership. This is what we lack today. *The distempers afflicting public life today reflect a crisis of the postwar consensus, the weak gods of openness and weakening, not a crisis of liberalism, modernity, or the West.* The ways of thinking that became so influential after 1945 have become unworkable and at the same time obligatory. We need to recover the "we" that unites us, but the postwar consensus is an undying zombie. The West needs to restore a sense of transcendent purpose to public (and private) life. Our time— this century—begs for a politics of loyalty and solidarity, not openness and deconsolidation. We don't need more diversity and innovation. We need a home. And for that, we will require the return of the strong gods.

CHAPTER ONE

# The Postwar Consensus

O n October 1, 1990, George H. W. Bush addressed the United
Nations General Assembly in New York. A veteran of
World War II, the American president recalled "the fires of
an epic war" that "raged across two oceans and two continents." For
the men who led the Allied forces and those who fought under them,
preventing a return of global conflict was an overriding imperative.
The leaders of the triumphant forces gathered in San Francisco in
June 1945 to adopt the charter of the United Nations. As Bush
recalled, their goal was "to build a new kind of bridge: a bridge
between nations, a bridge that might help carry humankind from its
darkest hour to its brightest day."

The Cold War dampened the promise of those hopeful early days
after Germany and Japan had gone down to defeat. The long struggle
to contain Soviet aggression required the postwar generation to defer
its hopes for the inauguration of a new era of global cooperation and
peace. But the wheel of history turned yet again. "The Revolution of
'89 swept the world almost with a life of its own, carried by a new
breeze of freedom," Bush told the delegates gathered from around
the world. Some still resisted the spread of liberty. Saddam Hussein's

Iraq had recently invaded Kuwait, annexing that sovereign nation in a manner reminiscent of Hitler's aggression in the 1930s. Bush assured the world that the United States would not stand idly by. He promised to fight for "a new and different world." Dictators would not be permitted to control the future. The president raised his eyes to take in a bright new horizon: "I see a world of open borders, open trade, and, most importantly, open minds."

This charming formulation was not a novelty in 1990. It expressed the essence of the West's postwar consensus. The history of the first half of the twentieth century seemed to speak for itself: German militarism and the seduction of aggressive nationalism caused World War I; in the social disorder that followed the armistice, Mussolini rose to power as the supreme leader of a paramilitary political party; Nazism combined anti-Semitic animus with a cruel ideology of strength; and, of course, communism governed in the Soviet Union for decades, feeding on the same totalitarian temptations. The inescapable lesson, most came to believe, was that war and destruction arose from close-minded modes of life and thought.

The consensus that Bush represented so ably at the United Nations held that to combat these evils and ensure that they never return, we must banish narrow-mindedness and cultivate a spirit of openness. Instead of dogmatic convictions and passionate loyalties, we need a spirit of critical questioning. Rather than reinforcing dominant social norms, society should loosen up and allow for greater freedom and experimentation. The "animal spirits" of the economy need to be freed from oppressive regulations; borders should be porous and open to commerce; and cultures need to expand their imaginative boundaries to welcome the contributions of new peoples. The world benefits from creative innovation, not conventional thinking. The spirit of openness, not dutiful obedience, is what we must cultivate.

## The Open Society

George H. W. Bush was the quintessential establishment man. His views were moderate and conventional. When he praised open borders, open trade, and open minds, he was relying on an adjective that had acquired an entirely approbatory connotation in the postwar West. He could be confident that term would arouse warm feelings and evoke images of a peaceful and humane future.

The sources of Bush's confidence ran deep. While World War II still raged, Karl Popper, a philosopher of science, worked to complete *The Open Society and Its Enemies,* a two-volume diagnosis of the civilizational madness that led to the global conflict.[1] By Popper's reckoning, civilization faces a choice. We can live in a tribal or "closed society," characterized by deference to authority and the subordination of the interests of the individual to those of society, or we can break free from this "collectivist" impulse and build an "open society," one that "sets free the critical powers of man."[2] The future of the West depends upon choosing the latter, Popper argues.

The enormous influence of *The Open Society and Its Enemies* in the decade following World War II seems, at first glance, improbable. The first volume is dominated by a detailed and highly critical, even abusive, interpretation of Plato, while the second volume treats Hegel and Marx with equal severity. Popper digresses into philosophy of science, metaphysics, and other abstract topics. His prose is full of "isms" and reads like a technical work of academic philosophy. But Popper structures his treatise to serve a clear political imperative, giving urgency to the twists and turns of his analysis.

The imperative is bracingly simple: *Never again.* Never again shall we allow totalitarian governments to emerge. Never again shall societies reach a fever pitch of ideological fanaticism. Never again shall the furnaces of Auschwitz consume their victims. This imperative—*never again*—places stringent demands upon us. It requires Western civiliza-tion to attain self-critical maturity with courage and determination, which Popper hoped to exemplify with his full-throated attack on Plato, the founder of our philosophical tradition. We must banish the strong gods of the closed society and create a truly open one.

One of the strong gods that the nations of the West must over-come is the nation itself. We are tempted to imagine our collective life as in some sense sacred, giving the community a rightful claim upon our loyalty. Popper regards this as "magical" thinking, a form of "anti-humanitarian propaganda."[3] Only the individual is sacred. The state has limited purposes. Its role is practical, not metaphysical and sacred. The job of government is "the protection of that freedom which does not harm other citizens."[4] This is not a simple task. Pop-per recognizes that harms are complex, and their prevention can be difficult, especially when one considers international affairs. But the challenge is technical and social-scientific, not cultural and political-philosophical. Good governance means allowing "the institutional technologists" to manage the machinery of the state so that it serves the interests of everyone impartially.[5]

Popper knows that there will always be "state-worshippers" and other proponents of "collectivism." They are the cause of the world's troubles. Such people must be dealt with firmly; anyone who relishes his homeland and its history is a "racialist," according to Popper. The vice affects more than the German people. It is a present danger in every nation. One can see how Popper anticipates our own era and its paranoid rhetoric. If someone worries about the effects of immi-gration on his nation's culture, he is xenophobic. If he organizes a political party that seeks to restrict immigration, he is a fascist.

But why would anyone become a "state-worshipper," especially after witnessing the disastrous consequences of National Socialism? In *The Open Society*, Popper proposes a psychological explanation that has been widely adopted. Critical thinking is difficult to sustain, he observes. Intellectual adulthood can be painful. The same goes for the political maturity that embraces the duties of life in a culture of freedom. We feel a "strain," Popper hypothesizes, when we live in a society governed by "democracy and individualism."[6] The "collectivist" proponents of a "closed society" promise something easier. They offer a more comfortable existence. Social authority, like paternal authority, is attractive to the insecure and fearful. Intimidated by the personal responsibilities freedom brings, we long for the security of obedience; we desire to "escape from freedom," as the social psychologist Erich Fromm put it in the title of his influential explanation of the origins of Nazism published in 1941. The closed and tribal society is psychologically soothing and reassuring. It helps us avoid the tension of "an ever-widening field of personal decisions, with its problems and responsibilities."[7] We must strengthen ourselves against this temptation, Popper warns. We need to embrace our freedom with courage rather than deferring to authority out of cowardice. Only an open society can save us from the return of totalitarianism.

Popper appreciates the allure of the closed society. While Fromm focused on a psychological explanation, Popper sought to expose the intellectual sources of our tendency to give our loyalty to higher truths and greater powers. By his reckoning, the main streams of Western philosophy tempt us toward totalitarianism. The Greek tradition represented by Plato and Aristotle pursues what Popper calls an "oracular philosophy" that employs an "essentialist method."[8] The ambition of this kind of philosophy is metaphysical—to know the truth. And insofar as truth is known, it must be affirmed, which is to say obeyed.

Therein lies the danger. A metaphysically ambitious philosophy leads to "medieval authoritarianism," with its hierarchical culture of command and submission.[9] Popper sees any form of transcendence as implicitly totalitarian. The recognition of something higher than the individual sets up a suprapersonal authority. If I can know what it means to be human, then I have a standard by which to judge individual behavior, and it is just such a standard, Popper argues, that is characteristic of a closed society. Long before the invention of words such as "logocentrism," Popper denounced strong truth-claims as threats to freedom and midwives of totalitarianism.

Against the possibility of metaphysical knowledge, Popper endorses the nominalism of William of Ockham, the fourteenth-century Franciscan who argued that concepts such as "human nature" are not essences but merely linguistic conventions (*nomen*, "name," thus "nominalism"). By Popper's way of thinking, a "methodological nominalism" must play an important role in the reconstruction of Europe.[10] Its anti-metaphysical linguistic conventionalism, which prevents us from imagining we can grasp the truth with concepts, encourages modesty with respect to truth, a disposition we need if we are to develop an open society.

Popper theorized the progress of science in formal, procedural terms, trying to encapsulate it in the principle of falsification, which stipulates that beliefs, theories, and hypotheses can be held as true only if it is possible for evidence to come forth that can falsify them. In that sense, our theories are always tentative, never known as truth, strictly speaking, but only held as not-yet-falsified beliefs. Plato's metaphysics does not rise to this standard, Popper argues, nor do Hegel and Marx's theories of historical development. These seminal figures in the history of Western thought are "above" empirical testing, as are all other metaphysical or meta-historical theories.

The key to social progress is the restriction of truth-claims to those that are falsifiable, Popper insists, tossing out nearly all of what the West has regarded as religiously, culturally, and morally foundational. Thus he devotes a great deal of *The Open Society* to harsh criticisms of Plato and the metaphysical tradition more broadly. When informed social scientists are allowed to test their proposals in "free and open debate," then and only then can we make social progress, improving the material conditions of our fellow citizens, perfecting democracy, and expanding freedom.

Although his framework is different, Popper anticipates John Rawls, whose political philosophy became influential toward the end of the twentieth century. Rawls insists that we should not govern society in accord with metaphysical claims ("comprehensive doctrines"). Justice as fairness rules out strong truths, he argues, differing from Popper, who rejects metaphysical claims because they are not open to empirical falsification. But the overall stance is largely the same. According to Popper, the strong truths are strong gods. They command our loyalty rather than being open to critical questioning and empirical falsification. As a consequence, they pose a threat to liberal norms. They are enemies of an open society. We need "public reason," as Rawls would put it. This is an anti-metaphysical, procedural approach in which truth-claims are limited to what can be empirically assessed by those who have command of the relevant data. In Popper's terms, we don't need politics in the classical sense, which involves arguments about how we should live, for these arguments invariably outrun the domain of what can be subjected to social scientific analysis. Rather, our politics needs to "go small," as it were. It should be scientific, not metaphysical. "A social technology is needed whose results can be tested by social engineering."[11]

This seems to raise an important question: What is freedom for in a liberal, open society? Historically, the West has appealed to metaphysics and religion for answers. Popper is aware of this question, and he gives an existentialist answer of the sort that Jean-Paul Sartre, Albert Camus, and others would make popular in the early 1950s. We must accept the "strain" of freedom, the existential tension that comes from knowing that we must *decide for ourselves* the ends our freedom is to serve. It is up to us to define the truths that we need. As Popper emphasizes in italics, "*Although history has no meaning, we can give it meaning.*"[12] This self-chosen path will require courage, but it is unavoidable, Popper argues. The very truth about reality itself depends upon us: "Facts as such have no meaning; they gain it only through our decisions."[13]

Nietzsche thought it would take superhuman strength for someone self-consciously to give himself his *own* truth. Only a strong god—an *Übermensch*—can mint truths rather than discern and obey them. This is certainly not what Popper wants. His goal is modesty, not self-assertion. He therefore hedges, writing about "meaning" instead of "truth." In this he is characteristic of the postwar era, which is deflationary when it comes to truth, not relativistic in a thorough-going way. Value-free facts alone constitute the domain of truth in Popper's universe. Whatever we make of them amounts to "meaning." We are the sources of our "value" terms, which are distinct from facts and truth. Knowing this to be the case should make us modest in asserting our "values," which are only our opinions, after all. Popper thus neutralizes the strong god of truth, keeping it narrowly scientific. When we need a guiding and commanding language with which to govern our lives and set standards for society, we appeal to the weak god of "meaning."

Like so much else in *The Open Society and Its Enemies*, the shift from truth to meaning is required by the Manichean political choice that the catastrophes of the first half of the twentieth century seemed to press upon the West: either an open society or Auschwitz. In the face of such a choice, the desire for transcendent truth, once considered healthy, becomes a dangerous temptation. According to Popper, the quest for a higher truth "is born of fear, for it shrinks from realizing that we bear the ultimate responsibility even for the standards we choose."[14] Since we often cannot endure the "strain" of freedom, we are tempted to invent truths and pledge our troth to them, setting ourselves on the road back to totalitarianism. The only way to avoid this trap is to adopt the double pattern of weakening—going small with a value-free, fact-based truth and satisfying the larger needs of the human heart with an ambiguous rhetoric of meaning.

### Liberal and Progressive Adaptations

The two volumes of *The Open Society and Its Enemies* I have before me are a first edition, published in Great Britain in 1945 as Berlin lay in ruins and American soldiers liberated the Buchenwald concentration camp. The copyright page assures readers that the collective obligations of the war effort were observed: "This book is produced in complete conformity with the authorized economy standards." A signature on the flyleaf indicates that it was bought by James B. Conant, the president of Harvard University and one of the top civilian leaders of the Manhattan Project, which produced the atomic bombs dropped on Hiroshima and Nagasaki. His discrete markings in the margins indicate that he read the book with interest, especially the passages in which Popper expounds his conviction that an "attitude of reasonableness" must be the basis for a democratic society.

Conant, like Popper, trusted in science and believed in the intellectual virtues of impartiality, vigorous debate, and close attention to empirical data. Both men were champions of democracy, which for them meant a liberal, open society. The authoritarian regimes in Germany, Italy, and Japan had been defeated, but they both worried that a resurgence of authoritarianism posed the greatest threat to Western civilization and its moral achievements. They were not alone. The Soviet Union's aggressive stance in the aftermath of the war dramatized the ongoing threat of totalitarianism. Their counsel was vigilance in defense of the open society and a thoroughgoing cultural reconstruction to forestall the return of the strong gods.

Popper, perhaps more than Conant, was aware of the self-contradiction of this counsel. The intellectual foundations of the open society must not go too deep or exercise too powerful a hold over our imaginations lest the intrinsically authoritarian metaphysical tradition be awakened. The open society must be intellectually circumspect and self-denying, even when it comes to defending the sanctity of the individual, which the open society exists to promote. That sanctity must be asserted, but it cannot be defended in metaphysical terms.

The open society must be anti-metaphysical, though not in the doctrinal way that Nietzsche encouraged, for the assertion that truth is self-made is itself a strong claim, a heroic one, as Nietzsche recognized. Rather, the open society is the result of an ongoing critique and the rejection of strong claims of any sort. Popper offers exactly that in his accounts of Plato, Hegel, and Marx. Clearing the ground with his critique, he then occupies it with his own temporizing rhetoric, which alternates between fact-based truth and self-chosen meaning. In an open society, reason restricts itself to pragmatic, procedural, and data-driven analysis and argument, supplemented when necessary with "meaning" and other ambiguous terms. In this way, Popper hopes to encourage an enduring but non-metaphysical loyalty to the ideals of the open society.

Conant represented establishment American liberalism. Whether inspired by Popper or not, after World War II that species of liberalism moved in the direction of empiricism combined with a rhetorical defense of democracy and freedom that resolutely avoided their metaphysical foundations. As George Marsden explains in his account of postwar politics in the United States, *The Twilight of the American Enlightenment: The 1950s and the Crisis of Liberal Belief,* an older liberal consensus based on natural rights gave way to a liberal consensus about the importance of consensus.

Arthur Schlesinger Jr., a bestselling historian and establishment intellectual who did much to form governing opinion after World War II, outlined an American response to totalitarianism in his book *The Vital Center: The Politics of Freedom* (1949). Capitalism and technology, he argued, release modern man from his traditional social bonds, leaving him homeless and atomized—a condition similar to Popper's "strain" of freedom. Modern man, Schlesinger observes, is vulnerable to authoritarians who promise to restore national purpose or reestablish social solidarity around a collectivist economic model such as socialism. To meet this threat, Schlesinger proposes a liberal politics of mediation. True liberalism is committed to constitutional freedoms that protect the individual, but it also brings human intelligence to bear on capitalism, directing its creative power toward the common good. With this combination, Schlesinger promises to "restore the balance between individual and community." A sense of solidarity based on widely shared prosperity rather than on the strong gods will allow us to achieve a stable common life consistent with the individualism of an open society. Although Schlesinger was writing about American society after World War II, much of what he prescribes has been the postwar project of social democracy in Europe as well.

What principles will maintain the balance between individual interests and communal purpose? None, as it turns out. Schlesinger and his liberal comrades believed the democratic West needed to enter a new phase of civic life. In the past, men fought over religious convictions and moral principles. In the twentieth century, these battles took rigid, ideological forms, leading to the disasters of militarism, fascism, and communism that brought war and misery to millions. Americans avoided this fate because our liberalism is based on pragmatism and empiricism, or so Schlesinger argued. New Deal liberals in America intuitively found their way to Popper's conclusions. Responsible governance means discarding political ideologies and using the new social sciences to craft effective policies. Urban planning, economic management, and other technocratic enterprises were thought to transcend ideology because they were based on scientific rather than political principles.

Belief in a new, post-ideological way of life was widespread after World War II. Social scientists and psychologists such as Abraham Maslow, Karen Horney, Rollo May, and others may not have read Popper, but his ideas were in the air, and they developed his themes, casting them as timeless, empirical truths rather than historically conditioned responses to the crisis of the West in the first half of the twentieth century. They did not have the dangers of fascism directly in view. Instead, they were concerned about the bourgeois culture of middle-class America, which was thought to constrict the full expression of individuality. The middle-class milieu of the 1950s was defined as "conventionality"—the pyschosocial analogue to Popper's "closed society"—and deemed an impediment to personal growth and authenticity. To counter these consolidating pressures, the influential psychologists of the era articulated the therapeutic forms of an "open society." At the same time, the new pop psychology of "growth" and self-realization, following Popper, remained scrupulously anti-metaphysical, not explicitly but as part of the larger and increasingly powerful postwar consensus. In the postwar explosion of the literature of personal growth and self-discovery, a new therapeutic search for meaning supplanted the classical search for truth.

Just what we were to grow *toward* remained vague, as it must when metaphysical questions are held at bay. Many influential books of the 1950s deprecated conformism, consumerism, and mass culture, just as Popper attacked the philosophical tradition of the West.

But as in *The Open Society and Its Enemies*, the alternatives were mere platitudes, variations on the theme of "openness." Man is to progress toward "greater meaning," self-actualization, autonomy—"liberation enabling each of us to fulfill our capacity so as to be free to create within and around ourselves,"[15] as Hillary Rodham declared to her fellow graduates of Wellesley College in 1969. Lawrence Kohlberg's theory of moral development culminates in a post-conventional moral code that is at once deeply personal and universal. But precisely because it is post-conventional, one cannot teach young people the content of this code, the pinnacle of moral development—that would make it into a social convention. One can only urge young people in the direction of ever-greater "growth" and "development."

At first glance, it seems obvious that politics without principles and personal growth without determinate ends are by definition open and capacious, for there is no basis on which to exclude particular ideas or initiatives. Consensus liberals like Schlesinger congratulated themselves for embodying that very openness. But in the main, consensus liberalism since 1945 has punished dissent, which it has consistently deplored as signaling a return of illiberalism, fascism, and other pre-1945 evils. The heightened rhetoric of anti-fascism should not surprise us. As Popper makes clear, pragmatism in politics—the end of strong truth-claims in public life—produces paradoxically powerful political and cultural imperatives. It *requires* denying principled political arguments and policies. Championing authenticity in personal life *demands* rejecting the authority of traditional moral norms. You can't lead young people to the "post-conventional" promised land without condemnations of "conventionalism."

This trajectory is evident in *The Open Society and Its Enemies*, which is full of passion. Popper's slashing and unmeasured criticisms of the metaphysical tradition of the West were a sign of what was to come. As the postwar consensus gained strength, it cultivated a purely critical faith, a negative piety. The "never-again" imperative imposes an overriding and unending duty to banish the traditionalists, who are loyal to the strong gods that are thought to have caused so much suffering and death. As the students rioting in Paris in 1968 insisted, "It is forbidden to forbid." Those who forbid must be censured and silenced—for the sake of an open society.

In retrospect, we can see political correctness at work already in the 1950s. Postwar liberals understood, however tentatively, that an open society is not self-inaugurating. It requires driving the strong gods out of public life and remaining on watch against their return. In 1955, Walter Lippmann, one of the most influential liberal journalists of the first half of the twentieth century, published *Essays in the Public Philosophy*,[16] a book he conceived in the dark days before the outbreak of World War II. As did Popper, Lippmann feared for the future of the West and its "traditions of civility." Unlike Popper, however, Lippmann urged a return to metaphysics to secure a stable basis for liberal society—respect for private property, free speech, and constitutional government. In our past, these commitments have been supported by a tacit but never fully elaborated public philosophy. Now, Lippmann argued, the future of free societies depends on making first principles explicit, which in his view means elaborating the natural-law basis for liberalism. We can best guard against totalitarianism when we know the transcendent sources of our political convictions. We need to attend to the deep truths that anchor the moral achievements of the West rather than banish them.

Lippmann was a journalist, not a philosopher, and *Essays in the Public Philosophy* features more exhortation than analysis. Nevertheless, anyone who has read Alasdair MacIntyre's *After Virtue* gets the gist of Lippmann's argument. The "public interest" was a term much favored by postwar liberals, who imagined it to be an empirical concept, the content of which can be filled in by social-scientific studies.

But the public interest is first and foremost an ethical-political concept, not an empirical one. We cannot promote the public interest unless we understand what man requires to flourish in society. Pragmatism and Popper's "social technology" shorn of metaphysics cannot tell us, which means we cannot maintain a liberal society solely on the basis of fact-based social policy and a consensus about "openness." We need solid convictions about what it means to be human so that we can discern what to be open *to*, for we cannot be open to everything. After all, the whole point of postwar reconstruction was to close off the possibility of a repetition of the catastrophe that wrecked the West between 1914 and 1945.

Today's readers are likely to find Lippmann's proposals vague and anodyne. Yet the liberals of the 1950s attacked him. The *New Republic* (a magazine Lippmann helped found) called *Essays in the Public Philosophy* the book of a "badly frightened man." In a six-thousand-word rebuttal in the *Yale Review*, Archibald MacLeish accused Lippmann of leading a "retreat from the idea of freedom" and of supporting the black-and-white mentality that undergirds McCarthyism, then as now American liberals' favorite synecdoche of totalitarianism. Other reviewers read Lippmann's appeal to natural law as an instance of "authoritarian" backsliding.[17] They were echoing Popper, though almost certainly unconsciously. The establishment liberals of the 1950s were criticizing Lippmann for failing, in effect, to adhere to the emerging postwar consensus. Too great an emphasis on truth, they presumed, leads to the ideological mindset and thus to incipient totalitarianism. An open society must be true to openness above all, not to truth.

The outlines of Popper's anti-totalitarian analysis were found not only in mainstream liberalism; progressives and socialists took it up as well, not because they read him themselves but because of the larger shifts in sentiment caused by the catastrophic events between

1914 and 1945. In 1943, two psychologists at the University of California launched a project to study the roots of anti-Semitism. They, too, wished to prevent the return of totalitarianism, racial animus, and nationalist aggression. In short order, they enlisted two refugees from Nazi persecution, Else Frenkel-Brunswik and Theodor W. Adorno, the latter a leading figure in the Frankfurt School, a Marxist group of anti-fascist intellectuals who fled to the United States during the war. Max Horkheimer, another member of the Frankfurt School, joined as head of the growing research team. They did not use Popper's closed-versus-open terminology, favoring instead the distinction between the "prejudiced" mentality, which makes one hostile to those of different races and religions, and the "unprejudiced," liberal mentality, which fosters a more welcoming attitude. The resulting volume, published in 1950, proclaims in its title their diagnosis of the great evil that World War II was fought to overcome: *The Authoritarian Personality*.[18]

"No politico-social trend imposes a graver threat to our traditional values and institutions than does fascism," the authors declare.[19] Although fascism was defeated on the battlefield, the danger remains. Western societies are full of "potential fascists," people with a propensity to "antidemocratic thought." To meet this threat, the authors of *The Authoritarian Personality* put their social-scientific training to work, conducting surveys and interviews of Americans of various backgrounds with the goal of answering two key questions: What makes a person a "potential fascist"? and How can we prevent young people in the United States from being socialized into the authoritarian mindset?

*The Authoritarian Personality* is a long, sprawling report, full of charts, correlations, and interview transcripts. A great deal of the analysis depends upon a now-discredited Freudian theory of psychological development. The survey questions are tendentious and today would not pass muster in an undergraduate class in social psychology. But seventy years later, these shortcomings are of no importance to us. What's striking is how familiar the analysis sounds. When the authors synthesize their results, they hit the notes of the emerging postwar consensus. The potential fascist is an American who was raised in a hierarchical family with black-and-white rules. His outlook on life is characterized by "conventionality" and "rigidity." He engages in right-versus-wrong thinking that supports "the dichotomous conception of sex roles and of moral values."[20] This potential fascist has a "prejudiced outlook," which conforms to the "ethnocentrist" mentality of the closed society. But the fascist mentality need not predominate. We have a different personality type in our midst, the authors observe. "There is a pattern characterized chiefly by affectionate, basically egalitarian, and permissive interpersonal relationships."[21] This personality type exhibits "greater flexibility" and adopts a more accepting disposition toward others. It embodies the virtues of an open society.

In the final paragraphs, the authors turn to the questions that haunted the years after 1945. How can we prevent another Auschwitz? How can we prevent World War III? Little can be done about adults who manifest "authoritarian personalities." Their attitudes have hardened. Attention turns, therefore, to children. Basic social institutions and norms need to be reconstructed in accord with new principles attuned to the dangers of a "prejudiced outlook" and the authoritarian personality. This fundamental change in the socialization of children will not be easy, the authors warn. "The problem is one which requires the efforts of all social scientists."[22] They must unite to develop "a scientific understanding of society" that diagnoses the bad effects of traditional social norms on the political-cultural tendencies of citizens. On the basis of what they imagined to be a scientific understanding of the roots of authoritarianism, bigotry, and fascism, progressive social scientists were commissioned to develop new anti-authoritarian norms and institutions.

The authors of *The Authoritarian Personality* did not call for a coercive campaign of social reconstruction, "however well-grounded in modern psychology the devices of manipulation might be."[23] Their hopes were akin to Popper's. They wanted to use human intelligence to guide, not command, society toward "openness." People are to be encouraged, not required, to develop a capacity "to see themselves and to be themselves."[24]

Like Popper, the researchers who contributed to *The Authoritarian Personality* seek to cultivate what can be called a negative piety, which gives priority to critique and self-questioning over conviction. This negative piety guards against resurgent authoritarianism by renouncing metaphysical claims. There can be no substantive end or purpose to life. After all, someone who defines an end or purpose for man becomes a black-and-white thinker, a potential fascist. Like Arthur Schlesinger and the consensus liberals, the authors of *The Authoritarian Personality* rely on warm gestures and open-ended ideals—"behaving realistically," achieving "self-insight," and "being fully aware." Such phrases, right out of Popper's lexicon, are versions of the postwar rhetoric that develops open-ended, fuzzy substitutes for words such as virtue and truth.

*The Authoritarian Personality* proposes pedagogies of freedom designed to liberate men from the psychological oppression of self-limiting prejudices and personality traits. Some social engineering may be needed, the authors allow, and the political correctness of our present era is latent in *The Authoritarian Personality*. The very title expresses anti-fascist aggression. But the ambition is negative and open, seeking meaning and "realism," not truth. Young people need to be liberated from restrictive, punitive ideas about sex, the researchers argue, as well as overwrought patriotism and ready appeals to authority. They call for a new consensus, the open society consensus, which will allow the next generation to live more naturally, more humanly, and more peacefully, freeing the West from its long history of hate, oppression, and war. It was new gospel, and it won many believers.

## Spontaneous Order

Karl Popper was not a conservative, if by that term we mean a defender of the old social hierarchies. He was an enemy of the sacred politics of tradition and a proponent of purely rational approaches to governance. Nor was he an old-fashioned liberal, a champion of nineteenth-century laissez-faire economics. Active in Austrian socialist parties as a young man, Popper was eventually repelled by the dogmatism of Marxism. Nevertheless, he maintained a generally progressive outlook on economic and social life. George Soros was his student at the London School of Economics shortly after the end of World War II, and the name Soros chose for the main instrument of his political and social advocacy, the Open Society Institute, testifies to Popper's influence.

It is striking, therefore, that one of the heroes of postwar conservatism, the economist Friedrich Hayek, like Popper an Austrian who fled Nazism, arrived at a diagnosis of totalitarianism and a vision for the future of Western civilization akin to Popper's. They became friends, united by a commitment to individual freedom and a desire to prevent the return of authoritarianism. With others, Popper and Hayek founded the Mont Pelerin Society, a group of intellectuals committed to thinking through the principles for the reconstruction of the West that would protect and promote freedom.

As Popper was working on *The Open Society and Its Enemies*, Hayek was writing his own wartime book, *The Road to Serfdom*.[25] It, too, sought to guide the renewal of Europe after the defeat of fascism, hoping to forestall its return. Like Popper, Hayek sees an enduring totalitarian temptation: "It is necessary now to state the unpalatable truth that it is Germany whose fate we are in some danger of repeating."[26] Published in 1944, a year before *The Open Society*, Hayek's analysis, however, has a different feel. Unlike Popper, he does not take up arms against the history of Western philosophy. There are no long, detailed refutations of Plato and Hegel. An economist, Hayek maintained a narrower focus. During the war, the economy of Britain, where he then lived, was transformed into a command-and-control system with production quotas, rationing, price controls, and wage boards. Horrified to learn that many intellectual leaders in England wanted these measures, redirected to peacetime objectives, to continue after the war, he wrote *The Road to Serfdom* to warn against the totalitarian consequences of this course of action.

World War II was fought to defeat fascism. But what is the true nature of this enemy? Too many people imagine fascism as a backward-looking form of primitive tribalism. Hayek argues otherwise. In the late nineteenth and early twentieth centuries, Germany was the center of socialist thought, which Nazism adapted. While its goals were nationalist, not those of international socialism, it imagined, as did Marxism, that human reason was capable of mastering the complexities of modern industrial economies, reconstructing them so as to attain greater efficiency and unity of purpose. In the ideology of National Socialism, society is a vast machine that can be reengineered to better serve the "destiny" of the German people.

Such hubris cannot be sustained, Hayek argued. But something worse than hubris is at work in the drive for central planning. The socialist, whether nationalist or internationalist, is concerned with the "general welfare" or "common interests," a way of thinking Hayek calls "collectivism." The collectivist imagines society to be governed by powerful forces that merge individuals into a single "we." The purpose of the state is to serve the higher ends of the "we," to which the interests of the individual must be subordinated. This pattern of thinking about social and political life, argues Hayek, characterized Hitler's race-based fascism as well as communism's class-based total-itarianism, an analysis that made *The Road to Serfdom* influential in the postwar era.

According to Hayek, collectivism stands in contrast to the signal Western insight, beginning in the Renaissance, that the individual is the sacred center of culture. An individual's desires, needs, and inter-ests are the only social realities available for rational analysis, which must serve as the basis of responsible statesmanship. It is individual-ism, which he sometimes calls liberalism, that provides the proper social philosophy for those who wish to defend the West, and indi-vidualism stands opposed to collectivism.

Hayek is not as precise as Popper, but he intuits that resistance to collectivism requires an anti-metaphysical stance. Since the basic principle of individualism is individual liberty, we must resist any-thing that compels our choices, even holding at arm's length the com-pelling character of solid and significant moral truths. "There is noth-ing in the basic principles of liberalism to make it a stationary creed," Hayek writes.[27] The essence of individualism is the freedom of every individual to be "the ultimate judge of his ends."[28] I must have the liberty to decide what is good or bad *for me*. By "good or bad," the economist Hayek undoubtedly means increasing or reducing my util-ity rather than congruent with morality or not. Nevertheless, in a number of passages, Hayek, like Popper, treats metaphysical reali-ties—the social bond, moral truth—as threats to the individual. He, too, advocates a severe intellectual asceticism. Only the individual is real; notions such as the general interest and common good are, at best, placeholder terms for aggregations of individual interests and welfare. At their worse they are bewitching idols that become sources of tyranny.

Hayek's metaphysical minimalism stands in contrast to collectivism, which presumes "the existence of a complete ethical code in which all the different human values are allotted their due place."[29] A social philosophy of this sort marshals political and social pressure to bring individuals into conformity with what is purportedly good for *us*. If we allow ourselves to think in terms of the common good—or any substantive good—we are on the slippery slope to socialism and collectivism, the road to serfdom. Although he does not say it explicitly, Hayek implies that there is always greater freedom for the individual when the social consensus about right and wrong is weakened. The prerequisite of cultural deregulation and the reign of the weak gods was already evident in John Stuart Mill's defense of individualism, *On Liberty*, published nearly a century earlier.

Collectivism is an enemy not only of freedom but of world peace. Germany's aggression arose from the priority fascism gives to the "we," fostering an insular mentality that excludes others. "Indeed," writes Hayek, "the very concepts of humanity and therefore of any form of internationalism are entirely products of the individualist view of man, and there can be no place for them in a collectivist system of thought."[30] At every turn collectivism brings woe. It leads to economic inefficiency, oppression, and war.

Popper and Hayek champion the individual against the collective. Both suspect that strong metaphysical claims feed the totalitarian temptation. They insist that the future of the West depends on a renewed commitment to freedom—the open society. This does not mean they agree across the board, any more than the center-left and center-right expressions of the postwar consensus have agreed on social policies over the past seventy years. They differ in important ways—ways that illuminate the difference between postwar liberals and postwar conservatives.

Popper speaks warmly of "social technologists," who adopt an empirical approach to governance rather than a metaphysical one. The consensus liberals in the United States during the 1950s regarded their analysis of policy issues in just this way, as do many liberals today. Hayek, by contrast, offers a thoroughgoing criticism of the technocratic approach. He places Keynesian economists and progressive social scientists into the collectivist camp. By his way of thinking, the scientific planner—the "social technologist," to use Popper's term—is perhaps worse than the old-fashioned autocrat, for in traditional, pre-modern societies those in power lacked the technical means to control individuals. Today, however, there is a real danger that planners will use social science to design a top-to-bottom mechanism to govern society on supposedly rational principles.

Hayek, unlike Popper, therefore champions the "spontaneous forces of society" as the principle of social order in a free society, not experts. The marketplace is the paradigmatic instance of this kind of order, he argues, which is why Hayek became a hero for postwar conservatives in the United States. Individuals in free-market economies enter into a rule-based framework that enforces procedural fairness and evenhanded dealings. But these rules are formal and remain agnostic about the ends individuals seek. In a well-ordered framework, the price mechanism allows buyers to find sellers, and a mutually beneficial exchange takes place. Over the longer term, firms are established, individuals enter into employment contracts, and supply chains develop, resulting in a harmonious social order without the totalitarian temptation of state-sponsored planning. Hayek recognized that rules are necessary for stable, open, and fair markets. But the object of the rulemaking should be to secure the greatest possible individual freedom in competitive markets. He was in that sense a "minarchist," someone who thinks human dignity is best served by a minimal definition of overarching social principles. This minimalism subjects the free individual to the least degree of coercion. We must obey rules of fair play rather than seek stipulated ends. At the same time, this minimalism allows society to achieve the spontaneous order of a free economy, which is always more efficient at producing wealth than anything consciously planned or dictated by the authorities.

Hayek was concerned about the economic inefficiencies of central planning, but the first principle of his individualism was individual liberty, understood as the greatest possible scope for action, unhindered by transcendent obligations or the commands of higher authorities. The bulk of *The Road to Serfdom* is a defense of the free market against socialism not only because the free market is better at producing wealth but, more importantly, because economic freedom is the foundation of an open society. We should bring as much of civic life as possible under the dominion of spontaneous market-organized relations, he argued. The more the market rules, the safer we will be from totalitarian domination.

It is not surprising, then, that Hayek argues that the reconstruction of the West after the war should follow free-market principles. Like those in the 1990s who predicted that capitalism would bring democracy and freedom to China, Hayek believed that the market mechanism is intrinsically anti-totalitarian. It is "the only method by which our activities can be adjusted to each other without coercive or arbitrary intervention."[31] A market-based social order is therefore the most moral approach to public life. It will forestall the return of the strong gods and block the road to serfdom.

In the postwar era, the center-right has assumed various political forms. European Christian Democratic parties affirmed some of the collective elements of public life, as did the Republican Party in the

United States, though the latter focused on anticommunist patriotism, while the former adopted social security policies we associate with the Democratic Party. In spite of those differences, market expansion has been a defining priority for postwar conservatism across the board. The European center-right laid the foundations for open markets that evolved into the European Union. American and European center-right parties supported global economic liberalization after the fall of the Soviet Union, assuming that it would promote human rights and liberal democracy as well as general prosperity. Although terms such as "individualism" and "collectivism," with which Hayek framed his analysis in *The Road to Serfdom*, have fallen by the wayside, his basic approach still defines the right-leaning postwar consensus. Freedom, peace, and prosperity are best served by expanding the market's function as the source of social order.

## Conservative Adaptations

William F. Buckley Jr. was a proponent of Hayek's insights. His first book, *God and Man at Yale* (1951),[32] which took aim at the pedagogy of serfdom at his alma mater, lacks the analytical power and intellectual scope of Popper's and Hayek's classics, and it is dated, passing judgment on now-forgotten professors and syllabi. But Buckley's youthful polemic reveals how powerful the consensus in favor of an open society had become just six years after the war's end.

One of Buckley's main assertions is that postwar Yale subjected its undergraduates to collectivist propaganda, defying what he regarded as the American tradition of private property, entrepreneurial initiative, and rugged individualism. At the same time, Buckley criticized the climate of skepticism that undermined religious faith and discredited deference to the transcendent. This, too, worked against what he saw as the American tradition, which traces our unalienable rights to the decrees of "Nature" and "Nature's God," as the Declaration of Independence puts it.

Buckley's piety—patriotic and religious—distinguishes *God and Man at Yale* from *The Road to Serfdom*. Nevertheless, this first book by the postwar era's most influential American conservative journalist manifests a strong loyalty to the ideals of the open society. Though he thinks the atheists and collectivists on the Yale faculty are wrong, Buckley does not censure them for their erroneous beliefs. His point is subtler. The Yale classroom of his undergraduate days, he argues, was not an arena for free and open inquiry. The atheist faculty often expressed their views in the classroom. Their reading lists included Bertrand Russell and other famous unbelievers of the time. The faculty who were Christians, by contrast, rarely defended their faith, striving to maintain a scholarly objectivity. As a consequence, the educational atmosphere was strongly biased in favor of unbelief. This could not but socialize undergraduates toward a secularist outlook.

Buckley makes the same argument about economics at Yale. The problem was not that John Maynard Keynes was taught or that some instructors argued for industrial management and high taxes. The problem was that this view was taught nearly to the exclusion of laissez-faire positions. Again, he argues that when alternatives are suppressed education becomes one-sided. Buckley insists that he is not in favor of counter-propaganda. The modern student needs to know the arguments in favor of "collectivism," as he (following Hayek) calls theories that emphasize economic planning. But Yale betrays the American tradition of economic liberty, he argues, when it fails to offer its students extensive and sympathetic exposure to the arguments for what he calls "individualism" (again following Hayek).

Buckley knew that he would be attacked as an enemy of academic freedom. The most philosophically interesting chapter in *God and Man at Yale* anticipates this criticism and frames a series of responses.

An accomplished debater, Buckley runs through a number of refutations, showing that the notion of absolute academic freedom is incoherent. Who in the shadow of Auschwitz defends the right of professors to advocate fascism or anti-Semitism? He notes the absurdity of "openness" as the highest good in education, mocking the conceit that Yale should seek to hire someone to teach about communism who is agnostic about whether communism is right or wrong—as if the ideal teacher should be impartial and undecided about the most decisive question of his time.

Buckley deviates from Hayek at a crucial point, forthrightly positing that the fundamental mission of the university is to educate the rising generation in the truth. His frame of reference, like nearly everyone else's at that time, is the civilizational crisis of the previous decades: "The denial of truth in Italy and Germany, coupled with the refusal of Japan to ally herself with truth, resulted in a devastating world war."[33] In the war's aftermath, the Allied forces occupying Germany had no illusions. It would be absurd to accord "academic freedom" to those who wished to renew the Nazi cause. America, Buckley observes, is not Germany, and the situation is not dire. But the same principle holds. Educators have a duty to guide students toward what is right and true. As he puts it, "The most esteemed values, if they are to triumph, must have a helping hand at the educational level."[34]

With a debater's élan, Buckley quotes Yale's president, Charles Seymour. A newspaper reporter had asked the Ivy League eminence to clarify the obligations of educators. He said that Yale and other institutions should "train our youth in the understanding and practice of American democracy whether in the classroom or in our campus life."[35] *God and Man at Yale* was written under the assumption that "the understanding and practice of American democracy" rests on the twin foundations of Christian faith and economic individualism. Buckley therefore ends his youthful tract with a call to the alumni of Yale University to rise up and regain control of the institution, returning Yale to its great mission: training Yale undergraduates, the country's future leaders, in the understanding and practice of the American tradition of freedom and democracy.

*God and Man at Yale* made a stir when it was published, evoking hostile responses from the liberal establishment that ran Yale and the other elite institutions in postwar America. Buckley was not criticized for his free-market views, nor was he censured for his traditional beliefs about the divinity of Christ. What irked the liberal establishment was his assertion of these views and beliefs as solid truths. One reviewer insinuated that the book was colored by Buckley's "Roman Catholic point of view," which is based on authority, unlike Yale's Protestant heritage, which relies upon individual conscience. Another reviewer invoked the specter of totalitarianism: "The methods he proposes for his alma mater are precisely those employed in Italy, Germany, and Russia." Still another wrote, "The book is one which has the glow and appeal of a fiery cross on a hillside at night. There will undoubtedly be robed figures who gather to it, but the hoods will not be academic. They will cover the face." Thus was the young William F. Buckley denounced as an authoritarian, a fascist, and a racist—an enemy of the open society.[36]

Buckley resented these insinuations, insults, and accusations. Nearly two decades later, during a televised discussion about the 1968 Republican National Convention with Gore Vidal, he threated to punch his liberal interlocutor in the nose for calling him a "crypto-fascist." That charge and the earlier ones were absurd. There was never anything remotely authoritarian in William F. Buckley's worldview. His religious piety never turned into a political program. Indeed, it seems hardly to have influenced his political views. He was opposed to any aggrandizement of state power and mistrusted efforts to enforce moral norms by legal means. To be sure, his civic piety exercised a powerful influence on his politics, but he was a thoroughgoing American conservative whose patriotism took the form of a passionate love for the American culture of freedom.

The youthful author of *God and Man at Yale* misjudged the social realities of the postwar era. In the aftermath of worldwide depression, fascism, global war, and the rising threat of Soviet totalitarianism, the mainstream of America's leadership class adopted the views of Popper and Hayek. The postwar reconstruction of the West, they believed, required not the old pieties and time-honored truths but an entirely new mentality, one immune from the temptation of dogmas of any sort. So skepticism took priority over belief, the spirit of suspicion and critique over faith and piety. This consensus, already achieving dominance as Buckley was writing *God and Man at Yale*, refocused the attention of America's leadership class. The true threats were now seen to be strong truth-claims, metaphysical formulations, and appeals to the transcendent. The content of beliefs matters, of course, but of more concern is the firmness with which they are held. And so the reviewers of *God and Man at Yale*, determined that the strong gods never return, lumped the young Buckley in with Joseph Goebbels and the Grand Wizards of the KKK. Buckley spoke too confidently and made too many truth-claims.

It was not merely "liberals" who attacked Buckley, if by liberals we mean the grandees of Roosevelt and Truman's Democratic Party. Buckley's main allegations were correct: In the aftermath of World War II, many believed in the possibilities of economic management and government planning, and elites were shedding explicitly Christian commitments. But those were trends within a larger agreement about the future of the United States, one that encompassed the views of postwar Republicans as well as New Deal liberals. It was taken for granted that America must lead the "free world," serving as the exemplary open society. Debates raged about what it meant to be an open society. The postwar consensus did not put an end to partisan division. Republicans emphasized economic liberty, while the Democrats emphasized social freedoms. But these disagreements took place within a powerful consensus about the open society. As we have seen, this consensus can forcefully condemn even as it demurs about what should be commended. It condemns those who commend too warmly, labeling them crypto-fascists and avatars of the authoritarian personality.

William F. Buckley was a gifted rhetorician, and over time he adjusted. In his introduction to the twenty-fifth-anniversary edition of *God and Man at Yale*, he retracts nothing, but the tone is different. He draws attention to the illiberalism of the reviewers who had so shamelessly smeared him. The snide comments about his Catholicism, allusions to the Ku Klux Klan, and accusations that he was a fascist—by the mid-1970s these rhetorical excesses had become embarrassing for liberals. It was a reminder that the anti-anticommunists of the McCarthy era often trafficked in the kind of defamation they condemned, a foreshadowing of today's punitive political correctness.

More telling still, when he turns to his youthful call for Yale to reconsolidate around religious faith and economic individualism, Buckley adopts a fresh argument. His plan, he writes twenty-five years later, was for Yale, a private institution, to pursue its educational mission in its own way and to do so against the currents of society's political orthodoxies. Such a course of action would realize "the ideals of freedom and pluralism."[37] Freedom was always Buckley's priority. Pluralism, however, was new. He picked it up from the postwar consensus that banished the strong gods. Pluralism is a solvent. It disperses rather than concentrates. In essence, Buckley was now arguing that returning Yale to its conservative roots would enhance the diversity of the American educational ecosystem, contributing to an open society on the terms Popper and Hayek established.

I have no reason to think Buckley changed his mind about the sources of the civilizational crisis of the twentieth century. In all likelihood, he, like Lippmann, believed that the disasters of the first half of the century were caused by false and perverse ideologies, not an "authoritarian personality." And perhaps, like Lippmann, Buckley continued to believe that the only enduring protection against this peril is a strong and articulate culture of truth, not vague appeals to "openness," "diversity," and "inclusion," to say nothing of the vacuous therapeutic clichés about "growth" and "self-acceptance."

But Buckley was a public intellectual trying to persuade the American people to adopt the views he thought best served the commonweal. As early as *God and Man at Yale*, he intuited, at least in part, that he could engage in public life only if he adapted his arguments to the growing postwar consensus in favor of the open society. That meant no strong gods—no large truths, no common loves, and no commanding loyalties. Thus the appeal to pluralism and other themes of openness—not, for Buckley, as ends in themselves but as a tactic to give conservatives a place at the table.

Over time, the tactic became a strategy, and in American conservatism the open society and free economy overwhelmed whatever was solid and permanent. Arguments from truth became arguments from meaning—or arguments from "viewpoint diversity" or some other rhetoric of weakening drawn from the postwar consensus. On the American right that process was largely complete by the time George H. W. Bush sang the praises of open trade, open borders, and open minds to the gathered delegates of the United Nations.

CHAPTER TWO

# Therapies of Disenchantment

In February 1943, the German Sixth Army, surrounded outside Stalingrad, surrendered, ensuring Germany's eventual defeat, and the attention of the United States began to shift from winning the war to planning for what would come after. In the spring of 1943, James B. Conant appointed the University Committee on the Objectives of General Education in a Free Society, composed of twelve members of Harvard's faculty, to study the future of secondary and higher education. An accomplished scientist, Conant recognized the importance of technical and scientific training for consolidating American dominance in the postwar era. But he worried about the social and political challenges as well. Conant wanted an approach to education that could "both shape the future and secure the foundations of our free society." It was urgent, he thought, to make ordinary American citizens loyal to the principles of a democratic culture and to prepare America's leadership class to put those principles into action. In 1945, the Harvard committee published its conclusions under the title *General Education in a Free Society*.[1]

The committee grappled with the tension between educational continuity (required courses and predetermined content) and the freedom proper to the questioning mind. Since the Western tradition is itself the source of the ideals of a free society, the committee argued, it must be passed down to the next generation. But precisely because critical inquiry and freedom are crucial to the Western inheritance, we must avoid slavish devotion to the past. The prophets of the Old Testament and the philosophers of ancient Greece criticized the consensus of their times. We, too, in our own time and circumstances, need the liberty to meet new challenges and address new needs.

The Harvard committee worked to combine traditional content with a critical spirit. The education philosophy of the future, they observed, must "reconcile the sense of pattern and direction deriving from heritage with the sense of experiment and innovation deriving from science that they may exist fruitfully together."[2] The rising generation should be socialized into the Western tradition, which has religious as well as philosophical dimensions. The committee was not interested in mounting a frontal assault on the tradition, as did Popper in *The Open Society and Its Enemies*. Nor is there a hint in *General Education in a Free Society* of the multiculturalism that came later. Nevertheless, the committee members were anxious about authoritarianism. Throughout their report, they returned again and again to the vexed question of the proper role of inherited culture, always resorting to circumlocutions to avoid strong, anchoring words such as "truth." Their preference for subjective terms like "meaning" anticipated the literary developments of the 1950s.

The committee's educational solution was to put the great touchstones of Western culture at the center of liberal education: the Bible, Plato, Aristotle, Augustine, Luther, Descartes, Locke, and others. "Education in the great books is essentially an introduction of students to their heritage."[3] But piety toward the past must be open to critical engagement and development. The committee envisioned an education that was conventional in content but innovative in method.

Their goal was to "uphold at the same time tradition and experiment," or as they put it elsewhere, "change within commitment."⁴ Perhaps Popper was a bit too dismissive of Plato's achievement, but his approach, the committee seemed to think, was generally for the best. A questioning spirit should characterize the transmission of the Western tradition.

*General Education in a Free Society* was widely influential. Beginning in 1950, it was the basis for Harvard's general education scheme for its undergraduates and set the pattern for what became known as "Western Civ," a curricular mainstay for decades. The 1960s saw rebellions against requirements of all sorts, but the basic pattern endured. When I was an undergraduate in the late 1970s and early 1980s, we were trained in the tradition-and-experiment, change-within-commitment model of liberal education. We were told that liberal education meant acquiring a basic fluency in the classic texts of the Western canon: Plato to the present, as it was known. But this tradition was taken as a source of independently discerned "meaning," not inherited "truth." We were to engage the Western heritage to construct our own answers to life's big questions.

The tradition-and-experiment consensus was always unstable. The Harvard committee sought a delicate balance between the authority of great books and independence of critical questioning. But the latter enjoyed the prestige of moral progress, and over time it predominated. Even as I was graduating from college, the consensus was eroding, and battles over the Western canon erupted in the 1980s and 1990s. The tradition side of tradition-and-experiment fell by the wayside. Why should "dead white males" and their Western civilization be privileged? A new, multicultural vision of education would expose students to cultural pluralism and awaken them to the persistent racism, sexism, homophobia, and xenophobia supposedly encouraged by dominant strands of the Western tradition.

Some resisted, treating the onslaught of multiculturalism as a destructive revolution in liberal arts education. Books were written lamenting the radicalism of the professoriate and loss of traditional learning. Some rallied to defend the tradition side of tradition-and-experiment. E. D. Hirsch Jr.'s *Cultural Literacy* came out in 1987, as did Allan Bloom's blistering attack on the post-sixties culture of higher education, *The Closing of the American Mind*. But the establishment consensus had moved on from the cautious balancing of the 1945 Harvard report. The new multicultural agenda was largely understood as a natural development of the earlier approach. The race, class, and gender pedagogy was seen by the liberal educational establishment as the next stage of the ongoing effort to build an open society. The generation of faculty and administrators hired by those who had adopted the principles of *General Education for a Free Society* pledged in turn to hire racially and culturally diverse teachers, who were thought essential for an inclusive environment in which various perspectives could flourish. The goal was to promote an education culture of still greater critical questioning. From the 1980s onward, the consensus was that these changes were necessary to prevent our society from perpetuating racism, sexism, homophobia, and xenophobia—which is to say, falling back into the authoritarian personality and the closed society.

Multiculturalism extends well beyond higher education, usually under the name of "diversity." It is tempting, however, to overestimate its influence. Today, the great books of the Western tradition are more neglected than critiqued. In the 1960s, literary critics such as Jacques Barzun and Lionel Trilling commanded wide audiences. The graduates of the expanded postwar college and university system in those years looked to novels, and even poetry, for insight into the meaning of their lives. The cultural scene is very different in the twenty-first century. Few recent college graduates can name a living poet. We now turn to social psychology, brain science, evolutionary theory, and economics to understand our lives and our society. Science provides the tools to diagnose problems and formulate solutions, much as Popper had hoped. Devoid of transcendence, these ways of thinking are materialist, not in the moral sense of encouraging greed and consumption (though some do that too) but in the metaphysical sense of reducing human reality to instincts and biological processes. Why read Jane Austen when it's obvious that economic theory provides a more objective and reliable guide to the dating and marriage marketplace?

In my experience, hard-nosed economists have no time for multicultural nonsense, which seems little more than progressive political dogma dressed up in pseudo-academic regalia. The same goes for neurobiologists and social psychologists. I doubt Steven Pinker takes seriously the latest effusions of gender theory. I sympathize with this reaction, but in recent years I have noticed something. The economists, psychologists, and brain scientists don't criticize the transformation of humanistic study by postmodern theories and multicultural ideologies. You won't hear them regret the loss of Western Civ requirements or the expulsion of the Western canon. This indifference calls for explanation. What led to the ascendancy of multiculturalism? Tyler Cowen is eager to engage in the critical examination of many things, but not this question.

Over the last two generations, economists have developed rigorous methods for analyzing social interactions not immediately economic in nature, often shedding useful light on the subtle play of interests. Gary Becker modeled marriage and domestic life in economic terms. Public choice theory frames the political process in terms of self-interested transactions. It seems odd, therefore, that economists are not modeling the educational "market conditions" that have allowed multiculturalism to displace the old tradition-and-experiment approach.

Why no theories about the ideological marketplace in higher educa-tion, or for that matter in corporate America, which has adopted the language of multiculturalism as well?

On closer examination, the neglect is not so strange, for it accords with the postwar consensus. According to Popper and Hayek, an anti-totalitarian culture requires sidelining the strong convictions that arouse powerful loyalties. The Harvard committee wanted to retain tradition but to moderate its authority by shifting from *truth* to *meaning*, from *conviction* to *critical questioning*. The anti-meta-physical materialism of the social sciences, it turns out, is crucial for this shift. The reductive explanations of the social sciences neuter the existential power of truth. Beliefs and convictions become prefer-ences and interests. As a consequence, by the late twentieth century, the political-cultural significance of the social sciences, brain science, and sociobiology came to parallel rather than contradict the human-ities' preoccupation with race, class, and sex. Reducing the human condition to economic interests or "selfish genes" has the same polit-ical and cultural effect as multiculturalism. Both disenchant and weaken, serving the ideals of an open society.

This consistency isn't obvious. How does the vague relativism of multicultural ideology square with the social and human sciences, which aspire to empirical rigor? At that level, they are indeed at odds. We live historically, however, not philosophically. As the postwar era unfolded, Popper and Hayek's anti-totalitarian agenda advanced in two ways. The first was the way of critique, culminating in today's diffuse but powerful ideology of multiculturalism. The second was the way of reduction, showing that human affairs can be explained by material interests and biological processes that govern us by default. These paths—critique and reduction—are therapies of dis-enchantment required by the postwar consensus. They dominate intellectual life today for political-historical reasons, not because of an intrinsic intellectual advantage. We prize them because we believe they promote an open society.

## The Way of Critique

During World War II, Karl Popper had difficulty finding a publisher for *The Open Society and Its Enemies*. He had fled Austria ahead of the Nazi takeover in 1938, accepting an academic position in New Zealand. Wartime disruptions to communications and paper shortages made it hard to shop the manuscript. His difficulties were compounded by the hostile reactions of some scholars who reviewed the text for publishers. Popper's relentlessly critical treatment of Plato and Hegel struck otherwise sympathetic readers as disrespectful and destructive. How could a book that purports to guide the reconstruction of Western civilization recommend a thoroughgoing rejection of Plato, the founder of Western philosophy, and Hegel, one of our tradition's most brilliant modern exponents?

Popper responded with a short preface to *The Open Society and Its Enemies* explaining his approach. "If in this book harsh words are spoken about some of the greatest among the intellectual leaders of mankind, my motive is not, I hope, the wish to belittle them. It springs rather from my conviction that if we wish our civilization to survive we must break from the habit of deference to great men." His frontal attacks, he suggests, are necessary for the future of the democratic West. We must strip our inheritance of the vestiges of sacred authority that blinker men's reason, making them vulnerable to ideological fanaticism. It is not cultural or religious piety that is needed today, but rather independence and courageous criticism. An open society needs open minds. To foster them, we must free the rising generation from its deferential habits. Breaking the hold of the past is not easy, especially given the seductions of thinkers as deep and subtle as Plato and Hegel. The open society will therefore require a sustained pedagogy of disenchantment.

"Disenchantment" comes from the German sociologist Max Weber, who used the term to characterize the experience of living in a modern scientific age. Reason's explanatory power does not just banish the supernatural from everyday life. It drains away the substance of Western culture's beliefs in robust metaphysical truths. By Weber's way of thinking, facts are distinct from values. Analytical precision and technical expertise shed no light on moral truths. If we are to be genuinely scientific in our approach, we must adopt a Spartan restraint when it comes to answering pressing questions about how we are to live and what we are to live for.

Weber delivered his famous lecture "Science as a Vocation" at the University of Munich in 1917. The terrible slaughter of World War I still underway, Weber presented disenchantment as a hard fate. Modern man has no choice but to put aside religious claims and with them the old, metaphysical worldviews of the West. We must navigate through life by the cold light of scientific reason and govern societies in accord with empirical analysis of observable phenomena. Popper issued a similar call for the scientific reconstruction of society in *The Open Society and Its Enemies*. But after 1945 the tone and tenor of disenchantment evolved in a way quite different from Weber's sense of it in 1917. Instead of being seen as a hard, even bitter, fate, disenchantment came to be seen as redemptive. The postwar consensus embraced "critical thinking" as an indispensable cultural therapy, necessary to prevent the development of the authoritarian personality and forestall the return of totalitarianism.

The changed meaning of disenchantment was soon evident. In a 1970 book on Sigmund Freud, the French philosopher and literary critic Paul Ricoeur cast the Viennese psychiatrist and theorist of personality as a cultural ally of Karl Marx and Friedrich Nietzsche, calling them the "masters of suspicion." Their impulse was to look "under" common opinions and everyday experiences to see "what's really going on." When faced with religious belief and obedience, Marx explained religion as a promise of deferred satisfaction that shifts the attention of the oppressed away from their exploitation by the ruling class, redirecting it toward future rewards in heaven. As he put it, religion is the opium of the masses. Marx analyzes other aspects of morality and culture in similar ways. What look like high-minded ideals are in fact elements of a cultural regime that legitimates the dominion of capital over labor. If you go to a lecture on constitutional history or visit an art gallery, what you're "really" hearing and seeing are intellectual and aesthetic justifications for unjust economic relations.

In postwar Europe, Marx and communism enjoyed social prestige, but in the United States anticommunism exercised wide influence within the liberal establishment. Its democratic ethos and tradition of individualism were inhospitable to Marx's class analysis, which gained little traction in American public life. Freud was a different story. He had quite different assumptions about the powerful forces underlying human affairs, and his psychoanalytical method focused more on the individual and his psychological well-being. In the intellectual culture of 1950s America, therefore, Freud was a more influential master of suspicion than Marx. The first wave of anti-totalitarian disenchantment in America was therapeutic, not Marxist.

A scientist of the human condition, Freud assumed that the fundamental sources of society are biological. In *Civilization and Its Discontents*, a general theory of culture written late in life, Freud posited two main human instincts.[5] One seeks sexual satisfaction. The other is aggressive and seeks domination. Taken alone or together, neither conduces to the cooperation necessary for human beings to survive in the hostile conditions of life, much less flourish.

Over time, then, human culture has evolved modes of socialization that sublimate man's instinctual energies, redirecting them to the task of their own repression. Freud coined the term "super-ego" to describe this repressive agent. It is the voice of conscience but not the oracle of a higher law that calls us to live more nobly. Moral self-discipline is part of a complex economy of instinctual energy circling back upon itself in the form of cultural norms. What looks like a high ideal is in fact repressed sexual desire or the aggressive instinct transformed into a severe taskmaster.

Freud was a therapist, not a revolutionary. In *Civilization and Its Discontents*, he writes, "We are often obliged, for therapeutic reasons, to oppose the super-ego, and we endeavor to lower its demands."[6] There are times, he asserts, when patients are overcome by neuroses caused by too much repression. The process of psycho-analysis "names" the sources of this over-repression (anal fixation, Oedipal complex, and so forth). Bringing these sources of psychic distress to consciousness gives the patient cognitive command over his interior mental states, allowing him to moderate the distress they cause. Something similar might be necessary for societies as a whole, Freud argues. We need to use our knowledge of the psycho-dynamics of culture to temper a too-repressive sexual regime or an overly idealistic and punitive moral culture. The wise social engineer employs therapeutic tools to manage the interplay of prohibition and permission.

Freud often turns to market metaphors. "Happiness, in the reduced sense in which we recognize it as possible, is a problem of the economics of the individual's libido."[7] We can't just spend, spend, spend to satisfy our sexual or aggressive desires. We must make regular deposits of instinctual energy into the repressive institutions and disciplines necessary to maintain cultural norms. But not too many deposits! We don't want to end up with a culture that produces impoverished, threadbare emotional lives. What we need, therefore, is good technocratic management of psychic drives and cultural demands. The "yes" of instinctual satisfaction needs to be balanced with the "no" of its repression.

The management model of life and society operates widely today, especially in the artificial environment of the university, where a great deal of effort goes into establishing a bright line of consent to distinguish rightful from wrongful sexual relations. This effort to impose discipline reflects a desire to find a "no" that does not erode the general "yes" implied by the sexual revolution. Something similar happens with the #MeToo movement, which wants to re-regulate our sexual marketplace but not in ways that undermine the general norms of openness and permission. What's wanted is a meaningful "no" that limits male predation but nevertheless supports the overall "yes" that regards sex between consenting adults as healthy and affirming.

The ethos of therapeutic management was already latent in Conant's Harvard committee, affirming tradition and experiment, change within commitment. They, too, wanted the "no" of required content that would not erode the "yes" of critical freedom. As I have observed, it was an unstable balance, and instability characterized the 1950s at many levels. Remembered as a time of conformity, that decade was in truth a period of deep anxiety about excessive conformity and conventionality. In *The Lonely Crowd* (1950), the sociologist David Riesman and his co-authors, Nathan Glazer and Reuel Denney, analyzed the "other-directed," imitative impulses of modern man, which they saw as eroding autonomy and authentic life. William Whyte's *The Organization Man* (1956) worried that collectivist thinking was destroying the American character of rugged individualism and creativity. Sloan Wilson portrayed soulless conformism in his novel *The Man in the Gray Flannel Suit* (1955). French existentialists sold in translation. Hollywood featured youthful angst. A beatnik counterculture caught the public's imagination.

At nearly every juncture during the 1950s, the dominant liberal establishment interpreted personal and social problems as flowing from one or another pathology of the "closed society"—overly repressive norms, a middle-class culture that disapproved of the unconventional, and an uncritical acceptance of social mores, to say nothing of racism, anti-Semitism, and sexism. As a consequence, most establishment leaders thought we should relax our cultural super-ego, tilting in the direction of change rather than commitment, experiment rather than tradition, permission rather than discipline. Children require more freedom to find themselves. People must be encouraged to discern and develop more individualized moral outlooks. Commitment, yes, but bespoke, not mass-produced. The consensus was in favor of openness; conservatives and liberals differed not about whether to loosen up but about how much.

The traumas of 1914–1945 explain this consensus. The entire cultural establishment wanted to forestall the development of the authoritarian personality. There was an emphasis on authority in the initial stages of the postwar era, true, but not strongly imposed and always open to experimentation. Convinced that a free society requires a foundation in the Western tradition, Robert Maynard Hutchins, the famous president of the University of Chicago, launched an ambitious Great Books project for a mass audience. Yet he too tilted against authority, even as he commended authoritative texts. "The [great] books should speak for themselves," he wrote, "and the reader should decide for himself." Tradition, yes, but the free individual has the final say. "The task of interpretation and conclusion is his. This is the machinery and life of the Western tradition in the hands of free men."[8]

This was a dynamic tendency, not a stable position. The arrow of development always pointed toward more openness, more decon-solidation of old authorities, and more disenchantment, which is why the revolutionary rhetoric of the 1960s, while certainly disruptive, was more in continuity with the 1950s than in rebellion against it.

Norman O. Brown was a classicist by training and a mythmaker by instinct. Born in England in 1913, he immigrated to the United States in 1938. During World War II, he was a member of the Office of Strategic Services, the U.S. Army's intelligence operation and the precursor to the CIA. A man of the left, he regarded socialism as the answer to society's ills. But postwar America's rejection of economic transformation discouraged him, and Brown became convinced that the rot went much deeper than the exploitation of the working class. By the mid-1950s, a study of Freud funded by the Ford Foundation led him to the conclusion that the entire sweep of human history entailed a terrible sacrifice of human happiness for the sake of repres-sive culture. Freud, he thought, was too pessimistic, restricting him-self to the technocratic management of the instinctual economy of sexual desire and its repression, just as the Harvard committee was too cautious, seeking to finesse the balance of tradition with experi-mentation. Marx's utopianism inspired Brown. He envisioned the "abolition of repression" that would lead to "the resurrection of the body," his term for the establishment of instinctual satisfaction as the final test of social justice.

Brown laid out his Freud-inspired theory of culture in *Life Against Death: The Psychoanalytical Meaning of History*. Published in 1959 by a small university press, it struck a chord and sold by the tens of thou-sands. Brown applied the Freudian hermeneutics of suspicion to soci-ety, and did so with vigor. We prize "Western civilization" not because of its intrinsic merit, he argued, but because we cannot face our own finitude, a diagnosis akin to the "strain" Popper thought would tempt us back to the closed society. To avoid the pain of finitude, we bind ourselves in loyalty to something we imagine greater than ourselves. But this cannot bring happiness. The disciplines of economic life reflect a culture arrested in the "anal stage" of development. "Money is excrement," he explains. At every turn, Brown works to disenchant culture. It is, he argues, the artificial, repressive enemy of human vitality and spontaneity. Cultural norms are a disciplinary "death" that is opposed to the instinctual sources of "life."

It's easy to make fun of Norman O. Brown. He followed up *Life Against Death* with *Love's Body* in 1966, an even more urgent and utopian call for Dionysian ecstasies that he promised would deliver us from the arduous demands of culture. The later book became a cult classic for those who wanted to theorize the Summer of Love. In retrospect, however, Brown's season of fame followed a general pattern. Michel Foucault published his study of the evolution of the social treatment of mental illness, *Madness and Civilization*, around the same time. It adopted an entirely different set of categories for social analysis but arrived at pretty much the same conclusions about the stultifying, constraining, and life-denying role of cultural norms. The work of both authors resonated with the postwar consensus that had come to regard the cultural traditions of the West as a problem, even a curse, not a welcome inheritance. By Popper's reckoning, totalitarianism is in the DNA of Western philosophy. Mainstream educators did not take such a dire view, at least not at the outset of the postwar era. But they, too, were less than confident in the old traditions. It was not just an anxiety about suburban conformism that drove liberal elites in Brown's direction. Death camps and atomic bombs hung over Western culture. In postwar Europe, colonialism became a source of moral embarrassment and shame. In America, the legacies of slavery and Jim Crow sullied the nation's shared inheritance.

The tradition-and-experiment balance was doomed to give way to something more radical, of which Brown and Foucault were harbingers. By the late 1950s, Jacques Barzun observed that executives of the Ford Foundation—the quintessential establishment institution—shed their suits at the end of the workday, donned the clothes of the working class, and headed down to Greenwich Village to listen to folk bands. In his reflection on the emergence of a non-traditional society, *The Triumph of the Therapeutic: Uses of Faith after Freud* (1966), Philip Rieff pictured postwar men and women increasingly uncomfortable "inside the starched collar of culture." Soon enough, the constricting collar was taken off. By the late 1960s and early 1970s, Popper's open society had evolved to include open marriages, open drug use, and a general conviction that open discussion of the most intimate details of life would bring greater happiness and self-acceptance. Demands for an open and ever more non-Western literary canon, as well as other elements of multiculturalism, were only natural.

There was nothing inevitable about the 1960s. It is simply false to assert that, given the choice, human beings will opt for what is immediately pleasurable. Throwing off social norms and cultivating "individuality" are not natural impulses. On the contrary, as social animals we're inclined to live in accord with dominant opinion, as Popper recognized, which is why he made the open society an urgent project (and which is why it now requires the policing of political correctness). Neither inevitable nor natural, the trend toward liberation from traditional cultural norms took hold because it was mandated by the leading ideas of the postwar era.

Those who went to Woodstock were not in rebellion against their parents, at least not in any fundamental sense. They may have upset the tradition-and-experiment balance that so many establishment liberals hoped to maintain, but the young people of that decade were acting out the imperative of openness that underlay the uneasy settlements of the 1950s. The same holds for the women's movement, gay liberation, and now transgender rights. These causes were not immediately endorsed by the postwar establishment, but over time they have been accepted, even embraced, as part of the general, presumptively beneficent trend toward diversity, inclusion, and openness. The liberation movements that focus on individual empowerment have become integral to postwar aspirations for an anti-totalitarian society. They are seen as barriers against the reemergence of the authoritarian personality.

To understand the last seventy years, we need to grasp their paradoxical character. The *cultural* consensus of the postwar era consolidated around an ambivalence about culture that, over time, evolved into an *anti-cultural* outlook. Figures such as Popper and Hayek implied that the norms of the Western tradition are not entirely sound and humane. They were not alone in this suspicion, which is not surprising, given the civilizational disaster that struck between 1914 and 1945. The mainstream liberal establishment was cautious. It wished to manage the tension between tradition and experiment, but the dark shadow of totalitarianism gave the latter tremendous social power. The open mind—and, soon, the transgressive mind—was seen as the indispensable guardian of the open society.

This consensus in favor of disenchantment led to a psychological ambivalence in the minds of most educated Americans in the 1950s. They accepted their social roles as necessary. The old norms reasserted themselves with a special vigor after the war as people sought the relief of "normalcy" after two decades of economic and political tension. But at the same time, the postwar consensus was training them to regard "questioning," "spontaneity," and modes of anarchic self-expression as pathways to a more humane and just world. The 1960s were in fundamental continuity with the 1950s. The student radicals of the 1960s were socialized into the postwar consensus as children. In a sense, their rebellions expressed the conventional wisdom of the era, carrying forward the logic of an open society to its next and fuller stage. The late 1960s was a time of turmoil. Yet the liberal establishment soon digested the radical demands, eventually adopting them as its own and recasting these challenges to "the system" as new forms of the openness that it had been encouraging all along.

Today, nobody remembers Norman O. Brown's *Life Against Death* or speaks of his "body mysticism." Freud has been discredited as a social scientist. The Marxist utopianism that Brown reframed as a vision of the triumph of instinct (life) over cultural norms (death) holds little sway over our imaginations. Nevertheless, Brown outlined the basic program that still dominates culture in the West. We see it at work in postmodern academic theory, which reigns in universities and provides the intellectual underpinnings for multiculturalism. This theory teaches that social norms and cultural ideals are manifestations of primitive impulses and instinctual urges: sexual desires, will to power, self-interest, lust for domination, class oppression, and so forth. Even our selfish goals—to look thin or to dress for success— get analyzed as social constructs, serving, perhaps, to sustain patriarchy, "late capitalism," or cisgender dominance. At every turn, we analyze "down," beginning our critique of social reality with things that might attract our loyalty and devotion and analyzing downward to the low, the ugly, and the base. What is today called "critical thinking" amounts to a thoroughgoing therapy of disenchantment.

At the beginning of the twenty-first century, the Harvard faculty embarked on another revision of its general education requirements. Gone was the concern to maintain the continuity of the Western tradition. When it comes to humanistic study, no specific content plays a privileged role. Instead, students must acquire critical thinking skills. The *Final Report of the Task Force on General Education*

(2007) tells us that Harvard undergraduates should know how to "read" cultural and aesthetic expressions, whatever they may be. The rising generation of global leaders needs to "understand how meanings are produced and received." This requires developing the capacity to put all cultural artifacts "in context—to see how social, political, and economic, and cross-cultural conditions shape the production and reception of ideas and works of art."

These educational goals are widely shared clichés, not just at colleges and universities but throughout today's cultural establishment. They reflect conventional thinking, a straightforward evolution of the consensus developed half a century earlier. Today's pedagogy, like the tradition-and-experiment balance sought by the Harvard faculty in 1945, remains ordered to the needs of an open society. "The aim of a liberal education," we read from Harvard's 2007 report, "is to unsettle presumptions, to defamiliarize the familiar, to reveal what is going on beneath and behind appearances, to disorient young people."

To be an educated person today means acquiring the virtue of disenchantment. At this juncture young people arrive at universities with very little cultural knowledge for teachers to disabuse them of. Still, the imperative remains. The rising generation should be guided toward what Philip Rieff calls "deconversion," the condition of critical knowingness that makes us "faithless," not in the sense of believing nothing but of not believing anything strongly, which is to say "uncritically." This negative piety allows our leadership class to be impartial brokers in conflicts about substantive truths, or so we are told.

Whether in 1945, 1975, or 2015, the consensus has remained substantially the same. In the postwar era, we've been trained to believe that the future of humanity depends upon our ability to drain the enflaming power of traditional truth-claims from public life so that benighted peoples will not rally around old, divisive loyalties.

The political imperative has remained constant: We must drive out the strong gods from the West. We do so by relativizing them, putting them into their historical contexts, critiquing their xenophobic, patriarchal, cisgender, and racist legacies, and showing how they are products of a sociobiological process that produces in us a reptilian "tribal mind." The postwar consensus promises that these therapies of disenchantment will deter the citizens of the West from renewing their fealty to the strong gods.

The cultural imperatives follow. Artists need to cultivate transgression! Corporations must celebrate diversity! At every turn, strenuous effort is put into weakening consolidating institutions and convictions. Religious faith, patriotism, the marriage covenant—responsible, establishment people believe that their duty as citizens in an open society is to "problematize" these traditional loyalties. Educators and cultural leaders cannot always succeed. The less educated tend to cling to their guns and religion. But we need not despair. The ruling class, educated in how "meanings" are produced and sensitive to "historical and cultural context," will manage these loyalties with techniques of disenchantment. Trained in the "production of meaning," they will use multicultural themes and diversity-talk to draw the sting out of potential conflicts, drive old loyalties to the margins of respectability, and otherwise advance the cause of an open society and open minds.

## The Way of Reduction

At the conclusion of *The Road to Serfdom*, Hayek summarizes what he takes to be the essential truth that must be recognized if the West is to avoid falling back into another cycle of social crises and totalitarian responses. Writing about the peoples defeated in World War II but identifying a truth that he believes the victors, too, must acknowledge, he states, "What the German and Italian who have learned the lesson want above all is protection against the monster state—not grandiose schemes for organization on a colossal scale, but opportunity peacefully and in freedom to build up once more their own little worlds."[9] In our public affairs, we must renounce our desire for great things and transcendent vistas, seeking instead only "little worlds": decent health, a modicum of wealth, and ordinary pleasures. The free society requires *going small*.

In the immediate aftermath of the war, Albert Camus became one of the most widely read spokesmen for the "little worlds" that Hayek commends. *The Plague*, published in 1947, represents his contribution to the extensive postwar literature of anti-totalitarianism.[10] In the novel, Camus presents a narrative argument: We can resist totalitarian evil only if we seek solidarity in the ordinary realities of life. He preached a humanism of little worlds, an outlook that renounces the lure of transcendence that tempts us to try to live up to seemingly noble principles and grand ideals. Our ambition should be to honor ordinary life, not to sanctify or otherwise ennoble it.

*The Plague* is set in Oran, a city on the Algerian coast. It is smugly prosperous, ugly, and "completely modern," lacking a heroic tradition or remarkable inheritance. Into the city comes a deadly pestilence, a metaphor for the disease of fascism. But Camus, unlike Popper and Hayek, is not interested in diagnosing the causes of totalitarianism. The plague afflicts as a natural disaster, a bacillus carried by rats, not as an ideological disease. What interests Camus is resistance. How can we sustain our humanity in the face of implacable evil?

One of the minor characters, Father Paneloux, indicates the false path. At the outset of the plague, he tells his anxious congregation that their afflictions represent God's severe call for renewed religious zeal and heroic sacrifice. Yes, there will be great suffering, but the love of God is a "hard love," one that asks us to "aspire beyond ourselves" so that we can reach the "summit" of a "high and fearful vision."[11] On this "summit," he preaches, we will see God's great and holy purposes in what now seems like senseless suffering and death.

Jean Tarrou moves in a better direction but falls short. He works with the narrator, Dr. Bernard Rieux, in a voluntary sanitary squad that spearheads resistance to the plague, an allegorical version of the French Resistance cells during the Nazi occupation. Tarrou's father was a government prosecutor. The young Tarrou once went to court, where he witnessed his father sentencing a man to death. The horror of a system of justice based on capital punishment drove him to join a communist revolutionary cell as a young man. But after a few years of activism, he was required to witness the party-directed execution of a traitor to the revolution. Alienated from both the established system and revolutionary resistance, Tarrou declares himself a partisan of humanity, not a loyalist to any particular ideology. But he, too, aspires to a "summit" beyond himself. His principled commitment to "humanity" requires "tremendous will-power, a never ending tension of the mind."[12] Even philosophical humanism falls victim to the lure of transcendence.

The narrator, Dr. Rieux, does not ascend to any summits. His voice is cold, objective, and analytical, befitting a man of science. He warns readers that we are inclined to think of those who sacrifice their lives in resistance as performing "some heroic feat or memorable deed like those that thrill us in the chronicles of the past."[13] But that tradition, so powerful in the West, is untrustworthy. It burnishes memory and idealizes the past. In truth, our motives are always mixed, and those who resisted the plague had "no such great merit in doing as they did."[14] At most, they were animated by common decency. That's a baseline of humanity, Camus insists, not a heroic stance.

Rieux befriends Rambert, a visiting journalist stranded in Oran because of the plague. He joins the resistance as well, but reluctantly.

He does not seek to serve "humanity." Grand philanthropy is not his transcendent cause. He simply wants to escape and be reunited with his wife. Rieux encourages this desire. The proper end of life is ordinary and everyday—the "little world" Hayek commends—not "heroism and sanctity." Rieux is a doctor. It is his job to fight disease. "It was merely logical," he says of his own involvement.[15] Rambert, by contrast, is a journalist and husband. He rightly wants to return to the small pleasures of his private life, which are tangible and attainable, unlike the supposedly noble ideals we so often embrace to give life meaning and purpose.

Eventually, the plague ends. Rambert gets his wish. The quarantine is lifted and he is free to depart. Rieux walks in his native city as the people of Oran return to the streets to chat, drink, and pursue romance—the ordinary run of human affairs. This is the true triumph that Camus celebrates, a return to solidarity in the quotidian, a solidarity that does not seek to climb to the high, corrupting summit of religious faith, transcendent commitment, or ideological fervor.

Camus repeats some of the same themes in *The Fall*. The main character is a dissolute, Mephistophelian figure haunting the dark cellars of Amsterdam. He is a fallen man of prominence, once renowned as a lawyer who defended progressive causes. As he reports, this seemingly noble calling was corrupted by vanity. In his philosophical ardor for justice, he would picture himself standing "above." Fueled by self-complimenting idealism, he ascended to the "summit," sinning against the only source of human decency Camus imagines possible in a metaphysically barren world: an everyday solidarity in ordinary things. The primordial fall, Camus suggests, occurs when we seek to rise in loyalty to higher ideals. When we love something greater and nobler than our own little, private worlds we ascend to a "summit," betraying our shared humanity in the lowlands. We risk becoming moral monsters, imagining ourselves servants of something greater. Camus consistently implies that this is the true source of totalitarianism.

Camus engaged Christianity in complex and interesting ways, but taken as a whole (and especially in his influence on his readers), he was, I have long believed, one of the most effective anti-Christian polemicists of the twentieth century. He was not a high-minded rationalist like Richard Dawkins, who brings out the elaborate siege engines of critique to show that supernatural faith is irrational. As Camus knew, this is a strategy that substitutes faith in reason for faith in God, which in some instances can be an even more remote "summit" from which to look down on ordinary life. Camus portrays all forms of transcendence as a moral betrayal, whatever their sources. We must accept that we're prisoners in a disenchanted, meaning-vacant world. Those who try to escape to places of religious, metaphysical, or moral absolutes are traitors. In Camus's imagination, they will return as executioners, savagely imposing their "truths" on humanity.

So it was something of a shock when, some years ago, I heard an elderly Dominican give a lecture on Camus at Providence College in Rhode Island that portrayed the French existentialist as an exemplary Christian thinker. During the discussion that followed, I expressed my disagreement, saying that Camus was utterly opposed to transcendence of any sort, which is hardly an aid for someone seeking to grow in knowledge and love of God in our secular age. The priest was adamant, even angry: Camus was a secular saint who could do more to teach us how to live as Christians than most theologians.

The encounter baffled me at the time. But I can now see that Camus played an important role in the postwar era, a time in which Catholicism, too, worked to relax its strictures and make itself more open, "smaller," and more ordinary. It embraced a demotic vernacular version of the Mass and adopted a horizontal, this-worldly style of architecture for its churches. Some of the most influential documents of mid-century Catholicism advocated a close alliance with postwar humanism, so close that it could seem as though the Church's transcendent faith had been reframed as an immanent project of political liberation or personal self-discovery. Camus reinforced this theological consensus against strong, transcendent truths. He wished to redirect our loyalty to the small things of life. Sharing our little worlds with others is the surest path to moral integrity.

Camus reassured the postwar generation. His novels and nonfiction taught that strategies of disenchantment strengthened rather than weakened the moral culture of the West, making it intrinsically anti-totalitarian. Disenchantment is a blessing, not a curse. That explains why the elderly priest was so eager to draw the French writer into the Church's orbit. It's also why the Nobel committee awarded him the prize for literature in 1957 at age forty-four. Camus can be a charming writer, putting philosophical ideas into winsome narrative form, but he was hardly a great literary figure. He was, however, a person of immense cultural importance in the 1950s. In his prose, the anti-metaphysical therapies of disenchantment that so many regarded as necessary to drain away the energizing sources of ideology and authoritarianism became a noble enterprise, the very essence of true humanism. The smaller our worlds, the more vacant our metaphysical dreams, the more arid our moral vocabularies, the more peaceful, decent, and accepting we become. Camus was the poet who sang in praise of Hayek's anti-totalitarian vision.

Milton Friedman was an American version of Albert Camus. This seems an absurd claim. Camus was a moody French existentialist, while Friedman was a cheery libertarian economist. Camus, though a staunch critic of communism, was a man of the left. Friedman, an equally vigorous critic of communism, is regarded by many to be the paradigmatic right-wing ideologue. In truth, they had a great deal in common. Both were enemies of transcendence.

Friedman shared Camus's antipathy for high ideals and, like Camus, he believed in the moral importance of focusing on the quotidian. It was Friedman's ambition to build a culture of freedom by driving ambitious, authoritative norms out of public life. He expressed the conviction of many proponents of the free market that only by reorienting society toward the "little worlds" of individual interests coordinated by the market mechanism can we protect human dignity from the crushing, coercive threats of the totalitarian state.

Friedman's popular book *Capitalism and Freedom* (1962)[16] is a sustained argument for the virtues of the spontaneous order arising from free-market exchanges. At the outset, Friedman criticizes the famous line from John F. Kennedy's inaugural address, "Ask not what your country can do for you—ask what you can do for your country." It was a call for Americans to adopt a noble approach to public affairs, one oriented toward goods that transcend individual interests. But that's precisely the problem, notes Friedman. "Neither half of the statement expresses a relation of free men to a free society."[17] We should not look to the nation for paternalistic support; nor should we think that our country is "the master or deity" that we, the citizens, must serve. "To the free man, the country is the collection of individuals who compose it, not something over and above them."[18] In public life, we are not to imagine there are summits to which to climb.

The bulk of *Capitalism and Freedom* concerns specific policies that Friedman believes will promote greater wealth and more freedom for postwar Americans. The book shares Hayek's anti-totalitarian moral purpose. The great threat to freedom is government power, the monster state. By its nature, centralized authority must legislate for all citizens, the lawmaker standing above, judging for the community what is right and good, and then imposing that judgment on all. The dangers are obvious. If we vest our government with the power to organize society, we alienate our freedom to someone above us. There is great potential for abuse in this relationship, to say the least, and Friedman makes the commonsense observation that "coordination without coercion" is preferable to principles of social organization that require coercion.[19] As Henry David Thoreau observed, "The best government is that which governs least."

Aristotle held a similar view, though he drew conclusions quite different from those of Friedman and the classical liberal tradition. Aristotle saw that a free society requires well-trained citizens who are habituated to seek what is just. The more virtuous the populace, the less coercion will be needed. According to Aristotle and other classical thinkers, reality will always be imperfect. As James Madison noted, men are not angels, and so government coercion will always be necessary. Like Friedman, Madison was anxious about the abuse of government power. His proposed solution was a constitutional system of checks and balances that he hoped would reduce the chances of a particular faction's gaining full control of the power of the state. But checks and balances go only so far. Madison recognized that we cannot engineer a perfect balance of power in society. Thus, he held that a good society requires a modicum of virtue and restraint in its citizens. This classical view was widely held at the founding of the American Republic. As George Washington noted in his Farewell Address, religion and morality are "the great pillars of human happiness" and together serve as "the necessary spring of popular government."

No doubt Friedman appreciated the idea of checks and balances in the U.S. Constitution, but he embraced the postwar therapy of disenchantment rather than the older reliance on the backstop of religion and morality. His ambition was to reduce the need for civic virtue. Anticipating the liberal political theorist John Rawls, he notes that we tend to fight over political power because so much is at stake when the government is responsible for promoting virtue and defending civic ideals. Given citizens' inevitable disagreements over moral issues, "the use of political channels" to organize society in accord with higher principles "tends to strain the social cohesion for a stable society."[20] Friedman does not articulate what Rawls later defined as "public reason," but in a similar spirit he seeks to disenchant political debate by focusing on basic matters of shared utility. By his way of thinking, political wisdom restricts government regulation of society to a "limited range of issues," for "every extension of the range of issues for which explicit agreement is sought strains further the delicate threads that hold society together."[21] This threat to social concord should be avoided, for men are always divided by "fundamental differences in basic values," and if we allow too much morality into politics, we risk "religious and civil wars."[22]

According to Rawls, rigorous philosophical reflection brings us to see that we must keep our "basic values" out of politics. Justice, fully understood, means legislating in accord with reason and toward ends that all citizens can affirm, no matter what they believe about the higher purposes of life. In practice this means limiting public debate to concerns that arise in our own "little worlds" of private interest rather than in the larger worlds of religion, metaphysics, and virtue.

Friedman adopts a more practical approach, but he arrives at the same conclusion. Individuals hold a wide array of values and preferences, some of which are based on religious beliefs and moral convictions. When we enter into the marketplace, we can express those beliefs and convictions as personal preferences, which in turn can be satisfied through collaboration and exchange with others. The way toward greater freedom, then, is obvious: "The widespread use of the market reduces the strain on the social fabric by rendering conformity unnecessary with respect to any activities it encompasses."[23] In a real sense, the market is a vast and perfect system of checks and balances far more reliable than the wobbly machinery of the American Constitution. Expanding the role of free-market exchange as the principle for social organization becomes a moral imperative. "The wider the range of activities covered by the market, the fewer are the issues on which explicit political decisions are required and hence on which it is necessary to achieve agreement."[24] We are freer, less contentious, and more at peace to the degree that economics rather than politics rules. The market is a miraculous Leviathan. It seeks universal rule but never exercises authority.

A great deal of *Capitalism and Freedom* argues for the greater efficiency of market freedom as opposed to planning. This has become a standard argument from utility used by the postwar right and eventually adopted by the postwar left as well. Friedman also outlines, however, an economistic political philosophy that has become very influential. He echoes Hayek's emphasis on the moral miracle of the market—bringing spontaneous order to civic life through countless individual exchanges. The market is anarchic in the precise sense of that term: there is no moral ideal, principle, or value that rules "from above." The free market requires regulation in the form of clear rules against cheating, deception, or other impediments to informed, free participation, such as cartels, monopolies, and other suppressions of competition. Friedman's moral passion was directed to restricting government to that role, leaving as much as possible open to the anarchism of the market.

In this respect, his larger view of public life was similar to that of Camus, who also favored anarchism. Camus focused on minimizing cultural authority rather than governmental power. He was concerned to disenchant traditional norms so that we can find our own, personally tailored way in life. Friedman's concern was with government, not culture. He recognized that we need a modicum of political authority, if only to protect citizens from external threats and enforce the economic rules of the road. His goal, however, was to minimize the state, just as Camus's goal was to minimize the shaping power of cultural norms. Friedman urged the privatization of Social Security and other entitlements, turning the collective question of intergenerational solidarity into private decisions about how to invest our own money. *Capitalism and Freedom* proposed changing food and housing support for the poor, as well as other targeted programs, into lump-sum cash payments so that individuals can decide for themselves what best serves their interests.

These and other privatizations are not commended on grounds of efficiency alone. The reorganization of public life around the "little worlds" of individuals turns troublesome and divisive questions of collective responsibility and common goods into private affairs in which each person can decide in accord with his private values and preferences. Privatization, Friedman promises, will allow us to fend off political conflict and reduce the state. This will promote freedom and frustrate the tyrants who seek to oppress us, be they petty bureaucrats or demonic ideologues. Put more simply, Camus wanted to privatize the moral life, while Friedman wanted to privatize political life. In both instances, "going small" was thought to be the surest way to promote the ideals of an open society.

Anyone reading *Capitalism and Freedom* in the twenty-first century cannot help but be amazed at how many of Friedman's policy proposals have been adopted—the elimination of price controls on national currencies and the Earned Income Tax Credit, for example. Some states have adopted educational vouchers and other methods to promote school choice, a proposal that in the early 1960s seemed fantastical. In 2005, President George W. Bush outlined a plan to privatize Social Security. It failed but remains a talking point for American conservatives, as does Friedman's call for balanced government budgets. He urged the decriminalization of "crimes with no victims," and over the past half-century profanity, pornography, and sexual transgressions have been decriminalized. Friedman championed the decriminalization of drugs as well, which many states are now in the process of implementing.

Taken as a whole, Friedman's proposals are not easily characterized as right-wing or left-wing. American conservatives have embraced his market-enhancing ideas that bear on government spending, hoping that they will reduce the size of government and restore the older virtues of self-discipline, economic independence, and personal responsibility. Liberals have echoed Friedman's calls for getting government out of the business of cultural regulation. For the most part, the American left has led the way in eliminating blue laws, sodomy laws and other limits on sexual relations, government regulation of contraception, and abortion laws. Liberals have also promoted the relaxation of divorce laws, drug enforcement, and pornography restrictions, and they sometimes work for the normalization of "sex workers." Friedman's political ecumenism reveals an important commonality between the postwar right and left. The postwar right emphasizes economic deregulation and the need to open up more space for free economic choices, while the postwar left focuses on cultural deregulation, Camus's concern. But they are united in their pursuit of an open society, differing only in focus and emphasis.

These projects—economic deregulation and cultural deregulation—are not at odds with each other. They reinforce each other, as Friedman often noted. Both presume and encourage the therapies of disenchantment. After all, man is a social animal, as anyone who is

remotely observant recognizes. We are religious animals and philosophical animals, as well, drawn to greater loyalties, shared projects,
and higher aims, which Friedman, like the liberal tradition more
broadly, sees as a threat to social peace.

Popper and Hayek consistently regard our tendencies to solidarity and our drive toward transcendence as fundamental threats to
the open society. Popper noted the "strain" of life without transcendent truths, which is why he emphasized the therapy of critique.
Hayek's strand of postwar theory, which Friedman took up with
vigor, is less self-aware. It imagines a bright line separating private
beliefs and public agnosticism. Individual preferences can include
transcendent aspirations, but the market is indifferent. But the bright
line cannot be maintained. The miracle of spontaneous order requires
individuals acting *as* individuals in the marketplace. As soon as we
bond together to seek a common good or higher truth, we begin to
forge institutions and movements to organize social life in accord
with our convictions. These are non-market organizations that form
the nucleus of the "monster state."

The culture of freedom envisioned by Hayek and Friedman paradoxically encourages the careful and minute management of culture.
We must be educated to believe that there are no common goods,
only individual interests. In this pedagogy, the ideologies associated
with multiculturalism become allies, not enemies, of the postwar
conservatism Friedman inspired. They assist in the moral goal of
expanding market order, for they habituate us to believe that there
are no higher truths to rally around.

It is true that in the eyes of the modern economist, multiculturalism mischaracterizes the interests that give order to society. The cultural theorists think in collective terms: the interests of the powerful,
the interests of capital, the interests of the cisgendered, the interests of
white males, and so forth. But economists and multiculturalists both

pursue disenchantment, which transforms truth into meaning—and then meaning into preferences, impulses, and urges, which today's economists interpret in individualistic terms, unlike the proponents of multiculturalism. This difference is significant, but what they have in common is of overriding cultural-political importance. Both approaches pursue a reductive analysis that disenchants what our tradition proposes as transcendent and worthy objects of our loyalty and love. This disenchantment, all agree, is beneficial, for it forestalls the return of the strong gods.

## The Neo-Liberal Shaman

The French *littérateur* Jacques Derrida exercised a remarkable influence over American academic culture in the 1970s and 1980s. He is seen by many traditional academics as the evil mastermind behind the takeover of the humanities by "cultural theory," the highbrow form of multiculturalism. Others regard him as the high priest of progressive academic politics. In truth, Derrida was not a revolutionary. He wrote about canonical Western thinkers such as Descartes, Rousseau, Hegel, and Nietzsche, drawing criticism later in his career for being "mandarin" and "Eurocentric." But more important, Derrida was a theorist of the postwar consensus. His work and influence were profoundly conventional. He became famous because he made disenchantment the theoretical basis of culture, laying the foundations for the fusion of economic and cultural deregulation that characterizes mainstream, establishment politics today, whether center-right or center-left. Derrida's singular contribution was turning the historical contingency of the postwar consensus into a timeless, anti-metaphysical truth.

Most of Derrida's writings take the form of close analysis of individual authors or texts, performances that follow a script he called "deconstruction." He begins by identifying the author's enabling assumptions, then shows how these assumptions rest upon a "center," a metaphysical concept that gives the text under study "a fundamental immobility and a reassuring certitude."[25] The paradigmatic metaphysical claim, observes Derrida, is the Greek philosophical notion of "being as *presence*," but the claim also can be the definition of a *telos* (end) or *eidos* (idea), an account of the authority of God, history, human nature, or reason. Each of these can serve as the fixed center or basis of the argumentative structure that the author erects to press home conclusions that we are to accept on the strength and solidity of the underlying foundations. Having identified and elaborated on the author's "center," Derrida proceeds to open up the slippage, the equivocations, the ad hoc configurations—the "play"—that characterize every operative distinction and basic definition.

To take an obvious instance, what, exactly, does it mean to say, "Being is *presence*"? In *A Grammar of Assent*, John Henry Newman discusses in great detail the gap between what is argued and what is affirmed as true. Derrida covers the same ground, though in the distinctive context of postwar French structuralism, from which he draws material for some of the complex pseudo-technical vocabulary of deconstruction (and which he disrupts in delightful and convincing ways). It would serve no purpose to compare them, however. Newman wanted to understand the relation between how we argue and what we know. Derrida isn't interested in that at all. Instead, he wants to dismantle claims to knowledge and point the way toward a radically disenchanted world in which one cannot know anything stable, permanent, universal, or transcendent. He was a philosopher, yes, but more enduringly a cultural critic and prophet, a role he put on and took off in playful, teasing ways throughout his writings.

Derrida's methods of deconstruction seized the imaginations of American academics for reasons that should now be clear. In 1945, the Harvard committee based the future of a free society on the balance between tradition and experiment. Haunted by fears of totalitarianism, however, the postwar consensus could not help but favor experiment and openness. As translations of his work percolated through graduate programs in the 1970s and 1980s, Derrida's conclusions gained sway. They allowed literary scholars to teach the great books of the tradition in ways that show their foundations are always in "play." There is no need to balance tradition and experiment, for in Derrida's approach tradition can be "deconstructed," shown to be nothing more than past instances of "play" that have petrified into "great books."

Derrida allowed higher education to say that culture *is* disruption and transgression all the way down. It is not surprising, therefore, that the educational establishment has largely accommodated itself to cultural theory. Its radicalism is only apparent, not real. Derrida and others took the ideals of the open society articulated by Popper and Hayek (again, not directly, but out of the postwar consensus that dominated elite opinion) and turned them into the foundational principles of culture. Popper's tilt against deference becomes a celebration of transgression and "decentering," while Hayek's insights into the virtue of spontaneous order are raised to the higher pitch of metaphysical "play."

Like Weber, Derrida recognized that his therapies of disenchantment can bring sadness. There is a "Rousseaustic side" of our era that longs for a return to an integral unity based upon sacred authorities. Faced with "decentering," "the absent origin," and the "disruption of presence," we can feel "saddened, *negative*, nostalgic, guilty," as if we are losing noble truths and betraying higher duties.[26] Derrida recommends what he takes to be a better way. We need a society that is open all the way down. That can be found when we view disenchantment as opening the way for "the Nietzschean *affirmation*, that is the joyous affirmation of a world of signs without fault, without truth, and without origin which is offered to an active interpretation."²⁷ These words of consolation amount to a sophisticated, now politically confident restatement of Popper's urgent, almost panicked, assertion some two decades earlier: "Although history has no meaning, we can give it meaning."

The parallels to Friedman's economistic political philosophy are remarkable as well. According to Derrida, reality is ours to make anew. We should not seek a refounding of the West in accord with a new "*given*." That would reestablish the closed world of the old, discredited gods. What we need is something intrinsically open, a reality-based "*genetic* indetermination" and "*seminal* adventure."²⁸ In a word, *play*, literary postmodernism's formulation of the anarchic ideal that Hayek and Friedman saw in the spontaneous order of the free market.

And it has been so. Although it was not obvious at the time, Derrida's philosophy destroyed the intellectual credibility of Marxism. Popper recognized that dialectical materialism participates in the metaphysics of presence as deeply as does Platonism, taking transcendent, foundational truths of metaphysics out of the realm "above" and projecting them into the future as the end or goal of history, the transcendent "new future." Derrida avoided a direct engagement with Marxist dogmas. He was always careful to maintain his standing as a man of the left. But his method of deconstruction has obvious applications to Marx, demolishing its pretension to provide a science of history. Bernard-Henri Lévy studied philosophy at the École Normale Supérieure in the late 1960s and early 1970s, experiencing Derrida's pedagogy and influence firsthand. It was a time of intense ideological contestation, mostly revolving around sectarian debates about Marx and Marxism. Lévy recognized that the political implications of Derrida's methods were the source of his influence and fame.

"Everyone is talking of *going beyond* Marxism," he wrote in 1974. "Derrida is perhaps the first to *outflank* it."[29]

Derrida's services to the rising hegemony of neo-liberalism involved more than disarming its competitor. "Genetic indetermination" is a precise description of the purposeless direction of free-market exchanges unhindered by the ambitions of economic planners. What is the creative destruction of capitalism if not "seminal adventure"? And what are technologists and entrepreneurs if not exemplars of those who provide an "active interpretation" of a world without origins or ends? Derrida can seem complex, but his cultural role has been straightforward: He disenchants, and in so doing clears the way for the triumph of the "little worlds" of private interests to which the free market ministers so well in the postwar era. With a rhetoric and effectiveness far more powerful than anything of which Hayek or Friedman was capable, Derrida ensured that all this could happen unhindered by the "saddened, negative, nostalgic, guilty" sense of civic duty. His ambition was to demolish the lingering intuition that, perhaps, we have common duties and shared loyalties to something higher.

In the early 1970s, the Italian philosopher Augusto Del Noce already recognized that, contrary to its mythology, the rebellion of '68 was not revolutionary. The attacks on traditional authority led to liberations of many sorts, but they enhanced the therapies of disenchantment, clearing away older loyalties or devotions that impeded the expansion of market exchange and its reliance on spontaneous order. The women's movement freed women to pursue their own desires without the hindrance of older norms of motherhood and wifely duty. They entered labor markets in record numbers. Gay liberation was supposed to overturn the bourgeois order, but in fact the gay lifestyle has become the *ne plus ultra* of discerning taste and self-oriented consumption. An entire generation of high-achieving young

Americans has been trained in multiculturalism, hard and soft. They slot seamlessly into jobs as management consultants, investment bankers, and Silicon Valley technologists. The literary critic Terry Eagleton sees the consistency of what seems contradictory. Postmodernism's "nervousness of such concepts as truth has alarmed the bishops and charmed the business executives, just as its compulsion to place words like 'reality' in scare quotes unsettles the pious Bürger in the bosom of his family but is music to his ears in the advertising agency."[30]

Del Noce's explanation for the paradoxical role of postwar radicalism has many facets, but the basic insight is straightforward. At every juncture the rebellions sought inspiration "under," not "above." This is the pattern of disenchantment that Norman O. Brown theorized in the late 1950s and Derrida soon thereafter. The "spirit of '68" intensified the way of reduction. As Del Noce put it, in our time, "Truth must play second fiddle to life."[31] This explains why Tyler Cowen and others today who follow in Hayek and Friedman's tradition are undisturbed by multiculturalism. Derrida's deconstruction helps us make the transition from social animals defined by our bonds of loyalty to individuals who seek our marginal advantages in the marketplace.

"It is forbidden to forbid!" As I've noted, that was a slogan rioting students wrote on walls in Paris in May 1968. Friedman was more modest: When possible, it is better not to forbid. The difference between hyperbole and realism aside, the sentiments arise from the same postwar consensus. By the first decades of the twenty-first century, that consensus consolidated around a neo-liberal approach in Europe and the United States. Open markets are for the best. Open cultures are for the best. The German chancellor Angela Merkel was not alone in announcing that we have no alternative. Only an open semiotic system can clear space for us to affirm life. Only open trade will bring peace. Only open borders will bring saving diversity. Only open minds can stop the return of Auschwitz. There is simply no other way.

When intelligent, educated, and responsible people talk this way, we know that we've reached a dead end.

## CHAPTER THREE

# Weakening as Destiny

A few years ago I was invited to speak at a conference marking the fiftieth anniversary of James Burnham's *Suicide of the West: An Essay on the Meaning and Destiny of Liberalism*. In this minor classic, published in 1964, Burnham observed that the West had been losing ground to communism, not just territorially but culturally as well. Anti-Western sentiment, common in former colonies, was spreading to Europe and America, taking root in the progressive left. The problem was not just that Europeans were being tossed out of their former colonial possessions (a process encouraged by American foreign policy). More worrying to Burnham was the loss of morale and the declining confidence in the superiority of the West's political and economic achievements.

His despondence was understandable. As the 1950s ended, communist Russia and China projected ideological confidence. The Russians were ahead in the space race. China had fought the United States to standstill on the Korean peninsula earlier in the decade and was developing its own nuclear weapons. The communist confidence was contagious. Indigenous leaders of former African and Asian colonies joined what many thought would be the winning side, while the liberalism dominant in the West after World War II, by Burnham's reckoning, was crippled by guilt, promoting a softheaded optimism about the essential goodness of man. Liberalism sought "dialogue" when firm resistance was needed. It insisted on "fair procedures" rather than clear assertions of transcendent truths about the nature and destiny of man. It encouraged the cosmopolitan conviction that the nations of the West deserved no privileged standing and that their pretentions to superiority enflamed and antagonized their adversaries, impeding humanity's inevitable evolution toward greater global harmony and cooperation. These liberal beliefs were disarming the West, Burnham argued, causing its decline in global influence and prestige.

I looked forward to the conference. There was a great deal to discuss. Burnham was obviously wrong about the world in 1964. Communism certainly posed a dire threat, but the Cold War blinded Burnham to the obvious: Communism, an ideology born and bred in the West, became the most powerful tool of Western cultural imperialism throughout the world in the decades immediately following World War II, expanding the global influence of European culture. Mao's communist rule destroyed China's traditional Confucian culture, paving the way for Westernization. The totalitarian application of Marxist ideology did more to Westernize Russia than the policies of Peter the Great. It provided a distinctively Western ideology for many third-world revolutionaries who sought to overthrow ancient monarchies, tribal systems, and the remaining colonial administrative elites.

The pessimism that runs through *Suicide of the West* was contradicted by events. Twenty-five years after Burnham's civilizational obituary, it was the communist East that died. Yet his analysis remains a useful guide to the tone and tenor of liberalism. Nearly fifty years after the book's publication, his analysis could be applied to President Barack Obama's notorious "apology tour" of 2009, in which he sought to form stronger ties with a number of countries by frankly confessing America's failures. It was a "humble-brag" gambit, a series of truth-and-reconciliation gestures that made perfect sense in the liberal world Burnham dissected.

The book was remarkable for being both dated and timely, but I was more interested in an odd contradiction. On the one hand, Burnham juxtaposed the communist East with what was then called the "free world," assuming his readers' commitment to the West's open societies. Yet as he detailed what he took to be the suicidal weaknesses of Western liberalism, Burnham implicitly endorsed qualities found in abundance in 1960s communism. He argued for firm convictions (communist version: dialectical materialism) rather than mealymouthed relativism, affirmation of hierarchies (communist version: dictatorship of the proletariat) rather than an unworkable egalitarianism, hard-nosed realism and philosophical clarity (communist version: Marxist orthodoxies) rather than aimless pragmatism and the plastic rhetoric of the open society.

Burnham did not want his readers to become communists, of course. He wanted the West to recover a firm, principled self-confidence based on its conviction about the superiority of its way of life. Although he did not say so, Burnham sought a renewal of the West based on something like Walter Lippmann's call for reflection on the metaphysical foundations of a free society. Without this renewal, Burnham worried that postwar liberalism would decay into "a generalized hatred of Western civilization."[1] At bottom, his argument was that an open society required convictions strong enough to inspire the sacrifices necessary to defend it, convictions at least as strong as those that animated our communist adversaries during the Cold War.

All of this was swirling in my head as I prepared my notes for the conference. Burnham was one of the founding editors of *National*

*Review*, and the conference was organized by the William F. Buckley Program at Yale University, so it naturally featured conservative presentations and panelists. As the day unfolded, I was struck by the tenor of the discussion. There was no talk of "absolute duty," which Burnham regarded as necessary for stiffening the spine of the West. Nobody elaborated "an exalted vision of the meaning of history," which Burnham saw as an essential antidote to liberal pragmatism.[2] Instead, the discussion followed the contours typical of twenty-first-century American conservatism—the need for lower taxes, the perils of socialized medicine, and the damage inflicted by political correctness. One panelist spoke of the importance of "viewpoint diversity" in higher education. Another detailed the reasons why Obamacare is fiscally unsustainable. The horizon was libertarian, economistic, and utilitarian, far from the high matters of passionate loyalty Burnham thought so essential for the survival of the West.

As the day ended, I reflected on the irony of the event. *Suicide of the West* bemoans the existential weakness of postwar American liberals, a weakness that was encouraged by the shapers of the postwar consensus, who regarded metaphysical poverty as essential for the open society. Burnham, like Lippmann, dissented from that consensus. He sought metaphysical substance. But his twenty-first-century admirers gathered at Yale concentrated on what "really matters"—mostly economic analysis and its "small worlds"—emphasizing a libertarian version of freedom. As one participant insisted in a particularly blunt intervention, "Economics decides everything." The metaphysical poverty that Karl Popper insisted upon characterizes today's conservatives. They, too, operate within the postwar consensus.

As I headed home from Yale, an important feature of postwar history became clear in my mind: The Cold War concentrated the energies of American liberals and conservatives, however much they differed. The threat of communism provided existential urgency and gave postwar politics a metaphysical density, mostly in the form of patriotic loyalty. Conventional histories treat Vietnam and the 1960s as the crucial moment when that density and loyalty were lost. I do not gainsay the importance of events that dismayed so many during that decade. But it is important to recognize that the priorities outlined by Popper and Hayek—cultural critique and reduction of everything to economic interests—were already at work. They impoverished the political and cultural imagination of postwar elites. It was this weakening that Burnham worried about in the early 1960s when he wrote *Suicide of the West*.

The West won the Cold War in 1989. This is not something Burnham expected, though I'm sure he would have been thrilled, as all of us were, when the Berlin Wall fell. Little did we know that the West's release from that life-and-death struggle would expose it to the full force of the postwar consensus and its hostility to the strong gods. Unrestrained by the existential threat of communism, the Western postwar consensus tended toward pure negation, leaving us a utopian dream of politics without transcendence, peace without unity, and justice without virtue.

## From Consensus to Destiny

It is perhaps an exaggeration to call Gianni Vattimo a philosopher. "Intellectual journalist" is a more accurate term, at least if we take it to describe someone who reports on the development, salience, and debasement of ideas in society (as I am trying to do). An Italian professor and sometime politician, Vattimo spent many years teaching "hermeneutic philosophy," a European tradition of highbrow interpretation of our present historical moment. As he puts it, philosophy seeks "ontologies of actuality," which means outlining the context for a philosophical discourse that makes sense here and now rather than discerning the permanent structures of human knowledge and experience. He does not argue that there are no such permanent structures, but he holds that seeking them invites meta-physical self-deceptions that get in the way of social progress.

One could say that Vattimo is a highbrow propagandist who engages in a politics of actuality. He does more than describe the current scene. He is a rhetorician who seeks to reinforce the postwar consensus by making anti-totalitarian openness foundational. As a consequence, he serves as a reliable guide to the establishment sensibilities that predominate today. Vattimo is not a great thinker, but he helps us see the direction the intellectual winds are blowing.

In the mid-1960s, as Burnham was writing his lament over the debilitating weaknesses of the West, a group of Protestant theologians were interpreting this weakening as a sign of Christianity's triumph. Called the "death of God" theologians, the Americans Paul van Buren, William Hamilton, and Thomas Altizer, the English New Testament scholar and Anglican bishop John A. T. Robinson, and others recast Christian teaching about the crucifixion and resurrection as a social-metaphysical drama of divine self-emptying and self-weakening. Before Christianity, they argued, man saw his finitude—his confinement to "little worlds"—as a crippling defect. So he oriented himself toward the transcendent God, seeking to overcome the limitations of creaturely existence through service to the divine. In Christ, this sense of defect and desire for transcendence is turned on its head. The essential Christian message is that the remote High God of our theistic imaginations became human and died, negating the "otherness" of the divine and refocusing the spiritual life on seeking community, justice, and love in this world, a "spirituality" not unlike that which made Camus so alluring as a secular saint. Christianity is therefore anti-religious, if by religion we mean an aspiration to transcendence. The true gospel of Christ crucified is not freedom from sin and death; it is freedom from the compulsive, world-denying search for the God above, a freedom that allows us to live for the sake of solidarity with each other in this world rather than aspiring to happiness in the next.

The death of God theology drew upon prewar antecedents. The famous Protestant theologian Karl Barth insisted that Christianity is not a religion, by which he meant that Christian teaching contradicts our natural religious habit of serving a remote, transcendent deity. God, according to Barth, transcends our ideas of God, especially the metaphysical principle that the infinite cannot become finite, that God cannot become man. The proclamation of Christ explodes these metaphysical preconceptions. For a while, Rudolf Bultmann was allied with Barth against the pieties of liberal Protestantism. Like Barth, Bultmann emphasized disruption. Christ, he always insisted, is an "event." Divine revelation cannot be categorized or domesticated to serve as the basis or foundation of a stable religious or metaphysical worldview. The death of God theologians applied these ideas, arguing that God-as-object-of-worship domesticates the Christian revolution, which is one of inner-worldly transformation, not otherworldly aspiration. God is the "event" of his own self-transcendence. In his "death" he gives up his lordship "above" for the sake of love's triumph "below."

With a magpie's instinct, Vattimo picks up these themes without any apparent knowledge of their sources in twentieth-century Protestant theology—a sign of how congenial to the postwar consensus the ideas of these radical theologians always were, even as they were regarded as shocking and new in the 1960s. Vattimo argues that we can no longer believe in the "metaphysics of presences." (It is a signal characteristic of "hermeneutic philosophy" to say we can no longer believe in something rather than arguing that it is false.) The metaphysics of presence seeks a foundational "substance" on which to base our view of truth, relying on what Popper called an "oracular philosophy," which purports to see the essence of things. Like Popper, Vattimo regards this pretension as "authoritarian." And like the postwar generation as a whole, Vattimo takes it as axiomatic that anything that can be called authoritarian must be rejected. As he reports, we no longer want to live in a society governed by strong structures and rigorous norms. We prefer weak and open-ended thinking. In pursuit of an antiauthoritarian culture, says Vattimo, our era has embraced a metaphysics of "event" rather than substance. Truth is found in the openness of the "now" rather than in what is enduring and unchanging.

Vattimo offers a revisionist account of the West's religious inheritance in *After Christianity*, attempting to articulate a philosophical and religious way of thinking that will support an antiauthoritarian outlook, a spiritual approach based on "event" rather than "substance." He proposes a "spiritual" interpretation of the Bible rather than a "literal" one, a morality based on love rather than rules, and the abandonment of the missionary attitude traditionally associated with Christianity. In keeping with the death of God theologians, Vattimo interprets the secularization of postwar European societies as the triumph of Christianity, not its failure. In the contemporary West, Christianity realizes its inner truth as the "event" of "weakening." The gospel message of charity, re-envisioned as affirmation, inclusion, and acceptance, displaces the older religious morality based on strong truths. As Vattimo puts it, "If there is salvation somewhere, it has the features of lightening rather than justice."[3] We know the Kingdom of God has arrived when the church no longer exists. It will be a sign that boundaries between the sacred and profane have been erased: God is in all, and all are in God.

"Lightening" and "weakening" are useful metaphors. They capture the atmosphere of the postwar consensus nicely. Our moment is not one of thoroughgoing relativism or strict renunciation of moral principles. Instead, it encourages ways of thinking and social norms that are less burdened with pressing truths, giving us more elbow room to formulate our own bespoke views of the meaning of life while draining the demanding passions out of public affairs. The postwar political establishment, center-right just as much as center-left, has adopted the consensus view that this "weakening" is to be encouraged. It makes us less likely to rally around collective loyalties that fuel an aggressive politics prone to conflict and conducive to oppressive measures. The analysis one finds in *The Authoritarian Personality* has become common sense.

The metaphors of lightening and weakening recur throughout Vattimo's writings. The good news of our time, he insists, is the "weakening of Being," an omnibus formulation meant to capture the general trend toward openness, a vision of life unimpeded by boundaries or limits. Our collective projects are also portrayed as borderless and without a normative, authoritative center. Whether one thinks the news good or bad, Vattimo is certainly correct to identify the "weakening of Being" as the cultural-political project of our time. The educational culture of the West manifests a pattern of weakening. We no longer think of higher education as the source of strong truths. It is instead devoted to critique and reduction. An educated person in the twenty-first-century West is an expert at unmasking pretentions to transcendent truth, exposing them as instruments of economic competition, class domination, patriarchy, and white privilege, or as products of the blind struggle of our genes to survive.

These modes of analysis are not false, but they lead us "down." The unmasking turns our attention to small truths that do not shine and tempt us with passionate convictions. To explain patriotism as a function of the "tribal mind," for example, redirects our attention from something strong—the commanding claims of a higher loyalty—to the social implications of our DNA. We pronounce the sociobiological dynamic of clan behavior inevitable—programmed into our mental software, as it were. But the implicit genetic determinism does not maintain a strong hold over our moral imaginations. On the contrary, in contrast to the stories of famous patriots that often rouse our passions, talk of the "tribal mind" offers us something we can coldly analyze and efficiently manage. The metaphysical effect is "lightening."

The same pattern of weakening marked the work of the American pragmatist Richard Rorty, who took a decidedly anti-metaphysical approach, defining truth as "what your contemporaries let you get away with saying." There's something right about this formulation. Viewed sociologically, what counts as truth depends on the social consensus. When everyone (or nearly everyone) agreed that the earth was at the center of the cosmos, it was taken to be the truth of the matter. But according to the ancient Greek philosophers and the Old Testament prophets, what most people believe is not a reliable standard of truth. We need to base our claims about truth in something more trustworthy than dominant opinion. The Western philosophical tradition is filled with tussles over how to characterize that which is finally trustworthy—and how to conform our thinking to it.

Rorty does not dissent from this tradition, at least not directly. He modifies it. Like Socrates, he thinks most people are captive to false opinions. In Rorty's case, however, the most destructive false opinion is philosophical: Most people naively imagine that truth rests on metaphysical foundations. Rorty understood his vocation, therefore, as an inversion of Socrates's—liberating us from our native (but misguided) belief that we should seek strong, stable truths. This liberation, Rorty believed, allows us to act more realistically and humanely. Knowing that our truths are weak, not strong, and based in ongoing, open-ended conversation, not solid intuitions of permanent things, we will promote the virtues of an open society. In this way, Rorty contributed directly to the anti-metaphysical dimension of the postwar consensus.

John Rawls arrives at the weakening of Being by different means. Defining justice as fairness, he stipulates that in a pluralistic society it's unfair to use the power of law to impose one among the many larger views of reality. Therefore, strong ways of thinking, or what Rawls calls "comprehensive doctrines," need to be kept out of politics. "Public reason" should govern public life, and public reason restricts itself to arguments that are open to everyone, which is to say data-based arguments that accord with Karl Popper's principle of social scientific governance.

As a philosopher, Rawls suffers from a scholasticism of his own invention. But his general approach, which accords well with the postwar consensus, has been widely influential: Job number one for responsible thinkers is to promote and sustain an open society, which entails the imperative of weakening, at least in public rhetoric. Abraham Lincoln once elevated the affairs of the nation by appealing to the Bible, but today we are told we need to restrict ourselves to universal truths of science, especially the social sciences, which purport to be value-neutral. The Rawlsian version of the weakening of Being encourages us to think and talk in terms of sociobiology (the "selfish gene" or "tribal mind"), economic modeling, or some other fact-based mode of analysis.

## Openness as Divine Decree

Like Popper and Hayek before him, as well as many other postwar theorists, Vattimo recognizes that the lightening of truth and the weakening of Being are "continuously exposed to the resurgence of metaphysical temptations."[4] Our innate desire for strong truths puts us at "risk of lapsing into fanaticism and intolerance"—the authoritarian personality that haunted the imagination of the postwar generation.[5] We must therefore remain vigilant. We must protect the open society from our instinctual desire for permanence. We must defend "a tolerance that, as it is easy to see, can only point to the weakening of the idea of truth, and ultimately of reality."[6] This is not to say that "everything goes." Vattimo does not endorse wholesale relativism. We need to organize society around a new, "soft" authority, fluid and open-ended: "communication, community, dialogue, consensus, democracy, etc."[7] These are the political and social forms of charity that foster a "moderate and generous" approach to life, as opposed to the older, rigid conceptions of justice. As these images and gestures accumulate, we can detect the outlines of what Pope Benedict XVI called the "dictatorship of relativism." This is a cultural-political program first and foremost, not a philosophical position. Vattimo envisions an ongoing process of weakening. By his reckoning—and again, this is entirely in accord with establishment opinion in the West in the early twenty-first century—responsible, forward-thinking people must regard this weakening as desirable, even obligatory. Society is ever better when it is ever more open.

As we have seen, the twentieth-century Protestant death of God theologians, as well as related figures, such as Rudolf Bultmann, who rose to extraordinary prominence in the postwar era, covered similar territory. They were theologians of openness. In the second half of the twentieth century, Bultmann's description of Christ as an "event" became a widespread verbal habit. Whether used consciously or simply adopted out of conformity to the academic discourse of the moment, it was a rhetorical device for weakening the authority of dogma. The Christ "event" does not endure. It always happens anew in the "now" of Christian proclamation, which bursts the boundaries of dogmatic and institutional constraint. By this way of thinking, authentic Christianity requires a spirituality of spontaneity and openness.

In the early 1960s, Joseph Fletcher developed "situation ethics." He argued that moral reasoning based on universal, authoritative principles leads to inhumane disregard for the unique and difficult circumstances people often face. What's needed is a more flexible approach, he argued, one that asks us to discern the loving response in unique situations rather than seeking to apply unbending rules. Indeed, sometimes what seems wrong is actually right. By Fletcher's way of thinking, it can be more loving to lie than to tell the truth. Adultery can be the most loving act, given the difficulties facing the spouse of someone who is incapacitated or abusive. Even murder can be justified in extraordinary situations. The point is not to throw up our hands and say that everything is permitted. Fletcher sought an approach to moral questions that relies on "dialogic mediation," to use Vattimo's formulation, rather than objective moral norms. We're to negotiate right and wrong with therapeutic nuance and attentiveness to the diversity of human needs.

The theologian Harvey Cox was another postwar theorist of openness. He rocketed to fame in 1965 with his book *The Secular City: Secularization and Urbanization in Theological Perspective*. As we saw with Camus, the postwar consensus encourages a this-worldly orientation. We are to "go small," not seeking transcendence but cultivating humane ways of living. Cox gained a large audience among upper-middle-class American Protestants because he explained how the postwar consensus fulfills rather than contradicts Christianity, reassuring American elites who were still loyal to Christianity. It was a relief to believe that the postwar embrace of weakening and the turn away from transcendence—away from the strong God who reveals strong truths—amounted to a paradoxical affirmation of Christianity. Unbelief became the fulfillment of faith.

The theological history of European Catholicism after World War II follows a similar path. One of the strong truths proclaimed by the

Catholic Church concerns our eternal destiny: There is no salvation outside the Church. After World War II, this dogmatic assertion became a topic of intense theological analysis. One of the most influential Catholic theologians of the postwar era, Karl Rahner, formulated a theory of "anonymous Christianity." The Gospel of Luke relates a colloquy between Jesus and the penitent thief who is crucified beside him. To the thief's plea to remember him when he enters into his kingdom, Christ replies, "Amen I say to you, today you will be with me in paradise." This passage was taken by Catholic tradition as warrant for thinking that the pious soul who desires union with God in charity but has not heard the preaching of the Church and has not had the opportunity to proclaim an explicit faith in Christ and receive baptism can nonetheless be saved. It is possible to be a hidden, or "anonymous," Christian. Rahner took this affirmation and expanded it. In the modern age, he argued, many who grow up in the shadow of Europe's cathedrals are unable to hear the Christian message for sociological reasons beyond their control. But insofar as they seek, in their hearts, union with God in charity, even unconsciously, they are in a sense already Christian. In this framework, a social conscience and philanthropic disposition can be taken as signs of desire for God, allowing us to regard all well-meaning, progressive people as quasi-Christian allies.

Just as Cox's message was a great reassurance to the American Protestant elite in the 1960s, Rahner's analysis was welcomed by postwar Catholic leaders throughout Europe. Prior to World War II, the Catholic Church tried to maintain a distinct political identity in Europe, establishing Catholic trade unions, newspapers, and political parties. Rahner's theory of anonymous Christianity (and his other reinterpretations of old dogmatic strictures) dovetailed with the postwar desire to reorient politics around a moral and political commitment to human dignity rather than divisive theological and transcendent affirmations. In the aftermath of the civilizational crisis that almost destroyed Europe, this shift toward open, non-dogmatic cooperation was felt to be of the utmost importance.

In the 1950s, '60s, and '70s, Catholic theologians, hoping to reduce Cold War tensions, entertained a new engagement with Marxism. The dialogue was alluring because it promised a this-worldly approach to public life that nevertheless preserved something of the strong truths, now seen as a quasi-transcendent commitment to social justice. One of Rahner's favored students, Johann Baptist Metz, transposed the crucifixion of Christ into a political theology that emphasized the disruptive and "dangerous memory of suffering" that explodes the structures of oppression.

By 1989, however, this and other forms of political theology in Western Christianity, like the Western humanistic Marxism from which it drew many of its concepts, was absorbed into the postwar consensus of generalized openness. Including the "marginalized" became the imperative of social justice, which requires breaking down "barriers" and overcoming "binaries." In progressive Catholic circles, the older Marxist utopianism became a utopianism of "dialogue," a world without "privilege" or hierarchy, without dogma, authority, or boundaries. In *Reflections on the Revolution in Europe: Immigration, Islam, and the West*, Christopher Caldwell reports the remarks of a European politician in the early twenty-first century: "We live in a borderless world in which our new mission is defending the border not of our countries but civility and human rights."[8] This is indistinguishable from the way in which some Catholic bishops in Europe now talk. The weakening of Being serves human dignity. It promotes the virtues of an open society—or so we are told.

Vattimo echoes these moves and many others in his revisionist account of Christianity. "Dialogue," "event," and "weakening" do not have technical meanings in the way Rahner's "anonymous

Christianity" has roots in the Catholic theological tradition. Vattimo proceeds by instinct, casting the postwar consensus in philosophical terms that serve as a cultural-political rhetoric rather than as rigorously thought-out concepts. His "metaphysics of actualities" reformulates the intellectual tradition of the West for our present moment, which he regards as requiring the ever greater openness that is the secular fulfillment of the perennial aspirations of the Christian West. It's a project that makes sense only in a cultural atmosphere dominated by the postwar consensus.

### Clearing Becomes Lightening

Vattimo's eclectic interpretation of the philosophical and theological traditions of the West is evident in his use of Martin Heidegger, a twentieth-century German philosopher who powerfully influenced continental European thought in the early decades of the postwar era. Having come of age before 1914, Heidegger, like Max Weber, regarded disenchantment as a cold, hard fate. The retreat of the strong gods from the culture of the West leaves a dangerous vacuum. Spiritually inarticulate, abandoned, and vulnerable, those living in a god-abandoned world seek the narcosis of spiritual self-deception, busyness, and—most tempting of all—technological mastery, a mentality that promises empowerment but turns everything into resources at hand for exploitation and control.

Heidegger was concerned about our penchant for self-assertion, our grasping efforts to fabricate spiritual-philosophical consolations—in effect, false gods—which can have practical-technical manifestations. Heidegger's outlook was strongly anti-American, regarding the United States as a soulless engine of production and consumption that threatened to overwhelm Europe with its cult of worldly success. But his lasting fame is the result of his analysis of the "metaphysics of presence," which he regarded as the perennial source of philosophical false gods.

Like Popper, Heidegger interpreted the controlling impulse to "see" as the defining feature of Western philosophy from Plato onward. But unlike Popper, Heidegger did not worry that this "oracular philosophy" exposes us to bewitching images of higher truths that evoke uncritical loyalty, the seeds of authoritarian societies. Instead, the "metaphysics of presence" pictures reality as "before us," available for our examination and manipulation. Put somewhat differently, Heidegger criticized the mainstream of Western philosophy (and theology) for being "theoretical" in a bad sense: eager to capture or encapsulate the essence of things in formulations that we can turn around and use to orient ourselves in the world. The "metaphysics of presence" is the foundation for our self-built house of knowledge.

Heidegger regards this dominant Western tradition—philosophy-as-technology going back to Plato—as the real source of disenchantment. The gods have not left modern man, he suggests in his often opaque and difficult reflections. Instead, modern man has been seduced by the metaphysics of presence, closing his eyes, stopping up his ears, and perverting the task of thinking. Instead of waiting, resting, and letting go of our desire for mastery, we have become relentlessly active. Instead of receiving truth as a gift, we transform our rational powers into manufacturing agencies that mint truth and declare it valid.

According to Heidegger, the task of philosophy is not to engineer a re-enchantment, as so many philosophers tried to do earlier in the modern era. Kant exalted the voice of conscience, which he saw breaching the divide between what is real (*noumena*) and our strategies for picturing and conceiving of reality (*phenomena*). Hegel turned our critical capacity into a sanctifying power. Insofar as we *see* the inner logic of history and the deeper historical meaning of

our cultural experiences, we realize and complete them. Later thinkers turned to will, intuition, and the soul's *élan vital*. In each case,
something within us erupts and floods the disenchanted world with
new urgencies and meanings. Against all these and other strategies,
Heidegger's ambition was to evoke a new mode of philosophy open
to the enchanting power of Being. He sought to still the grasping
impulse of the Western intellectual, allowing us to rest and harken
to the enrapturing power of Being that shines forth in every age,
including our own. The goal of true thought is "strengthening," not
"weakening." Philosophy truly practiced seeks to discern a cultural-
historical home in which to dwell, as it were, not to re-describe our
"lostness" and culture of negation as a happy destiny.

Vattimo turns the enigmatic German philosopher upside down,
as do so many postwar thinkers, such as Emmanuel Levinas and
Jacques Derrida. In the dark shadow of Auschwitz, almost all the
cultural leaders in the postwar generation treated disenchantment
as a divine blessing, not a hard fate. It delivers us from the strong
gods, securing the peace of indifference. As the 1960s bad boy Abbie
Hoffman put it, "God is dead and we did it for the kids." Heidegger
emphasized stillness, silence, and waiting. By contrast, Derrrida gives
priority to movement, the chattering interactions of texts, and play.
Heidegger speaks of thinking as entering into a "clearing," *Lichtung*
in German, which in its literal sense means "lighting," a place where
the light comes in. Vattimo turns this into "lightening," the reduction
of the weight of things that threatens to overburden us with convictions. Vattimo insists that the task of philosophy is to encourage the
weakening of Being, the very opposite of Heidegger's view that we
need to recover a re-weighted at-homeness.

One could examine this reversal in detail, working through the
appropriations of Heidegger by the postwar generation, especially in
France. I believe, however, that this brief description of how the

shapers of the postwar consensus turned Heidegger on his head is sufficient for my argument. Heidegger saw himself as a revolutionary thinker, on a par with Plato, whom he cast as the source of the Western philosophical tradition and the true origin of disenchantment, which Heidegger, like so many others of the pre-catastrophe generation, regarded as a burden and a threat to the future of Western civilization. In that sense, Heidegger's reading of Plato was not unlike Popper's. Both see metaphysics as a dire temptation, though with a crucial difference. Popper interpreted Plato in political terms. The Greek tradition of metaphysics is an "oracular philosophy" that purports to give us clear access to universal truths. Once we are convinced that we possess these truths, we will become moral monsters who seek to remake the world in accord with supposedly timeless truths. Whether it's Nazi race consciousness or Platonic contemplation of the Forms, the problem is the same. In both cases, Popper insists, metaphysical dogmas become false gods. In the frenzy of worshipful obedience we inhumanely seek to redesign humanity to fit what we imagine to be "essential." The remedy, held Popper, and the postwar consensus more broadly, is to banish the "essential," to drive the strong gods from Western culture. We must adopt a lighter, weaker sense of truth, based on trial and error, pragmatic adjustment, and empirical science.

This basic pattern of analysis—the source of totalitarianism is found in the impulse to reach for something greater, and the remedy lies in "going small" and adopting a weakening discourse—has been recapitulated countless times in the postwar era. Camus saw loyalty to something higher as a betrayal of the merely human. Milton Friedman worried that higher loyalties bring social discord, at least to the extent that they influence public affairs. John Rawls adopted a similar view. Comprehensive doctrines must be kept out of public life. Indeed, nearly all the leading intellectuals since 1945, left and right, have promoted the weakening of Being. The cultural-political project of the West should not be organized around strong gods, the postwar consensus has insisted.

The mainstream political outlook in the West has become more and more technocratic. We are told we need experts and scientists who can sort out a fact-based approach to life. Center-right opinion has tended to non-interventionism, using deregulation to clear space for spontaneous economic relations to govern benevolently. Center-left opinion has been more activist, emphasizing the work of "social technologists," as Popper described them. But both sides agree that politics should be based on economic, sociobiological, psychological, and other rigorous methods of analysis. To protect this project against metaphysical temptations, the postwar consensus has lauded shamans of transgression and encouraged a discourse of critique that unmasks: All truth-claims are historical, power relations shape the meta-narratives, and so forth. At every juncture our commitments need to be disenchanted—weakened and lightened.

Heidegger's interpretation of our times is more in line with Burnham's. Like Weber and Oswald Spengler, he could not convince himself that World War I's discrediting of traditional sacred authorities was a blessing. Heidegger attacks the metaphysics of presence because, by cutting us off from the power of Being, it thins out Western culture still further, leaving us destitute. Insofar as man is bewitched by metaphysics and its promise of a timeless template for understanding the world, he is encouraged to transfer the conditions for truth to himself, imagining that *he* possesses the key to knowledge, thus dooming himself to live in little worlds of his own making. And however well stocked these little worlds may be with the technological tools of mastery over nature, they are places of weakened Being. At best, we fabricate mental prosthetics to compensate for self-wrought disenchantment. Modern political ideologies are among those compensatory inventions, giving us the illusion of transcendence as we try to engineer a better future through activism.

In an important sense, Heidegger agrees with Popper. Totalitarianism arises out of a closed mentality, and the imperative of our age is indeed openness. But the cultural-political project that Popper inaugurated—a managed, orchestrated, and finally compelled openness—cannot achieve true openness, as today's political correctness makes clear. Nor can Vattimo's hermeneutical philosophy. The rhetoric of "weakening" dovetails with the neoliberal economic and cultural project of porous borders and infinite fluidity, a restless utopianism that is always looking for another boundary to overcome, as the present mania for transgenderism demonstrates. Rather, Heidegger commends spiritual openness. His later writings point to the need for serenity or "letting go," a disposition that opens the soul to receive the gathering, sheltering, and reconsolidating power of Being. We need to be rooted and at home, he insists on many occasions, not in fluid motion or engaged in "lightening."

Without the anchoring, abiding power of Being, we become interchangeable agents and subjects of endless manipulation—workers, consumers, buyers and sellers in the marketplaces of "identity." We engineer our lives, even choose our sex. But this freedom is exercised within the terms set by mass culture and the globalized economy. Professors market critiques. Artists sell transgressions. But these critiques and transgressions are integral parts of the postwar consensus, not "countercultural" at all, as is obvious when they are championed by elite institutions and rewarded with prestigious fellowships and prizes. Disrupting nothing other than what remains of the memory of the strong gods, they contribute to the weakening of Being, which is thought always to be morally salutary and necessary for an open society.

Vattimo has a genius for bringing out the defining features of the postwar West. Today our leaders treat disenchantment and weakening as great moral, cultural, and political achievements. "Lightening" earns the West its right to govern the world, for we do not come as arrogant, imperial patrons of strong truths, but as humble, almost belief-less, missionaries of the open society. Early in the postwar era, Philip Rieff recognized this spiritual self-praise in the ascendancy of a therapeutic mentality. In earlier times, human beings thought that happiness depended upon discerning truth and conforming one's life to it. Today, we speak of "healthy" beliefs, those which promote psychological well-being and social adjustment. The spirit of relativism that has character-ized so much of our culture in recent decades serves these therapeu-tic goals. Very few people entertain the notion that there are no truths. But we prefer soft truths, which allow us to affirm people as they wish to be affirmed. We withhold strong judgments, thinking it best if individuals are allowed to forge their own moral outlook and their own worldview. This therapeutic mentality is evident in the substitution, since 1945, of "meaning" for "truth," which the postwar consensus made inevitable. "Truth" has fixed and strong connotations. "Meaning" is personalized, mobile, and weak. The true saint of our time is a patron of meaning, not a martyr for truth. The man of mean-ing is our spiritual leader because he makes our society more welcom-ing, diverse, and inclusive.

Vattimo's signature image, the weakening of Being, transposes Popper's theme of openness into a quasi-metaphysical rhetoric that is more informal and accessible than Derrida's rigorous dialectic of deconstruction. Vattimo's emphasis on event provides another quasi-metaphysical popularization, capturing something of Hayek's and Friedman's love of the marketplace's miracle of spontaneous order. The free market is anarchistic in a precise sense: It has no *telos*, no higher purpose or ultimate end. It depends on nothing substantial and relies on no essence other than man's desire to maximize his utility. This desire for greater personal utility is a truth about the human condition, to be sure. But it is a small one and does not implicate us in the transcendent. Economic analysis will not draw us out of ourselves and direct us toward greater loyalties. As theorized by Hayek and Friedman, the order provided by the free market is an "event." The countless private decisions in the marketplace exist in the Eternal Now, to use Paul Tillich's term for divine revelation, another influential instance of the theological reformulation of the postwar consensus.

Vattimo recapitulates the postwar diagnosis of totalitarianism, scaling it up to a universal theory of the origin of evil not unlike the analysis found in *The Authoritarian Personality*. "Violence," he writes, "ultimately draws from the need, the resolve, and the desire to reach and be taken up into the first principle."[9] We oppress, harm, and kill only insofar as we seek transcendence and the arresting power of truth. "Weakening" is thus deliverance from evil; "lightening" is the salvation promised by the postwar consensus. Unwittingly echoing Tillich, Vattimo suggests that lack of faith is actually the most reliable sign of a deeper faith. It shows that we are not committing the sin of loyalty to an "objectifying metaphysics." True faith shuns strong truths and embraces the weakening of Being. It is not pride that goes before the fall, thinks Vattimo, but rather loyalty, devotion, and conviction. This is the paradoxically strong conviction about the danger of strong convictions that animates the postwar consensus.

I was grateful when Gianni Vattimo's work fell into my hands more than a dozen years ago, for he helped me see the underlying logic of the predominant cultural consensus that I find increasingly dysfunctional and oppressive. Vattimo takes the cultural and economic ideas for the reconstruction of the West that were developed in response to the civilizational disaster of 1914–1945 and turns them into an anti-metaphysical "destiny." He is correct, at least as far as recent decades are concerned. Weakening has been the trajectory of the postwar West, especially since 1989. The postwar consensus has calcified into dogmas of openness, so much so that some political leaders in Europe and the United States find it difficult to articulate a socially respectable rationale for border controls and immigration laws that were regarded as commonsensical a generation ago. The weakening of Being has become the obligatory way of thinking. The postwar consensus cannot imagine its own failure, its own contingency. It imagines itself the final, essential form of our liberal tradition and the culmination of modernity's achievements—our "destiny."

Although Burnham wrote *Suicide of the West* as a polemic against the liberalism of his day, the book is best read today as a warning against the enervating dangers of the postwar consensus. He agreed with the consensus's major premise: We should resist totalitarianism in all its guises. But Burnham intuited that, taken alone, the postwar liberalism of "openness" (Popper) leads to the diffusion of collective energies and the weakening of strong, concentrating loyalties. The same could be said for the romance with "spontaneous order" (Hayek) that was a prominent feature of the conservative movement of which Burnham himself was a part. As he observed, most of the liberals of his day were anti-anticommunists. They ardently opposed anything "strong," even strong denunciations of communism, which they too rejected, worrying that in anything strong lay the seeds of an authoritarian personality. In the place of traditional loyalties to "God, king, honor, country" and "a sense of absolute duty or an exalted vision of the meaning of history," liberalism "proposes a set of pale and bloodless abstractions." We are told to rally around "dialogue," the United Nations, "progress," and this or that program of the modern welfare state. Is it then surprising, he asks, that some people say "Better Red than Dead"? Only a fool dies for small things and "little worlds," for greater utility or procedural goods such as "free and open debate."[10]

Burnham was an American conservative, which means he was concerned to defend the American liberal tradition, broadly understood. In the early 1960s, however, he articulated the important insight that no culture survives without strong gods. This is as true for an open society as a traditional one. A society lives on answers, not merely questions; convictions, not simply opinions. The political and cultural crisis of the West today is the result of our refusal—perhaps incapacity—to honor the strong gods that stiffen the spine and inspire loyalty. We are subjected to the increasingly shrill insistence that "critical questioning" is the highest good and "diversity is our strength." We are told that every motif of weakening, dispersion, and disenchantment serves the common good because it forestalls the return of Hitler.

But we are not living in 1945. Our societies are not threatened by paramilitary organizations devoted to powerful ideologies. We do not face a totalitarian adversary with world-conquering ambitions. Insofar as there are totalitarian temptations in the West, they arise from the embattled postwar consensus, which is becoming increasingly punitive in the face of political populism and its rebellion against the dogmas of openness. Our problems are the opposite of those faced by the men who went to war to defeat Hitler. We are imperiled by a spiritual vacuum and the apathy it brings. The political culture of the West has become politically inert, winnowed down to technocratic management of private utilities and personal freedoms. Our danger is a dissolving society, not a closed one; the therapeutic personality, not the authoritarian one.

## CHAPTER FOUR

# The Homeless Society

W hen F. W. Woolworth set about to erect a monument to his success as a mass retailer, he commissioned the architect Cass Gilbert, an early-twentieth-century proponent of architecture that affirmed America's role as heir to the best European traditions. Gilbert was hardly an anti-modern man. When the Woolworth Building in New York was completed in 1912, it was the tallest in the world. Gilbert employed the latest technologies to construct something that would have been unimaginable only a decade earlier. Yet this emblem of progress is a neo-Gothic tower that evokes the great cathedrals of Europe. Woolworth and Gilbert affirmed the industrial age, but they knew that it rent the fabric of traditional society. Like the Harvard leaders in 1945 who wanted to balance tradition and continuity with critical questioning and change, the builders of the sixty-story tower sought a balance, embracing new possibilities and sustaining old forms. The same is true of the Chrysler Building. Completed in 1930, it surpassed the Woolworth Building in height, and its art deco style is more futuristic. But gargantuan stainless steel gargoyles, links to our cultural past, gaze out over the teeming streets of midtown Manhattan.

There were modernist rebels before World War II. The Swiss architect Le Corbusier insisted that twentieth-century Europe needed a decisive break with its architectural past, which he regarded as morally bankrupt. He advised bulldozing Paris and starting over again. But in the first decades of the twentieth century, his ways of thinking were countercultural and therefore marginal. After the war, however, the architectures of continuity gave way to those of discontinuity. Le Corbusier's views were ascendant. Theodor Adorno famously declared that there could be no poetry after Auschwitz. Brutalism, an aggressive style rendered in concrete, said the same thing about architecture, its angry pillbox ugliness announcing the impossibility of traditional beauty after 1945. We must not find repose in the familiarity and reassurance of tradition. To do so nurtures the authoritarian personality, or so we are told.

Man is not made to dwell in ruins, on a battlefield, or in a "machine for living." Brutalism faded, and elegant variants of modernism, its austere forms well suited to postwar anxiety about the strong gods, became the house style of corporations and governments throughout the West. Architectural modernism echoes Enlightenment ideals, emphasizing regularity, order, and unornamented forms. In expert hands, these principles can produce visually harmonious buildings with a clean aesthetic that sheds the weight of historical memory, which the postwar era felt more as a burden than a blessing. The minimalism of modernism invites different interpretations, embodying the ideal of openness.

Mies van der Rohe was a leading modernist, and the Seagram Building in New York is one of his masterpieces. It is not muscular like the Chrysler Building, nor is it a confection to delight the eye like the Woolworth Building. Standing in splendid, bronze-tinted elegance on Park Avenue, a timeless study in glass and steel, its clean lines bring pleasure to the eye. But it makes no historical claim on the storehouse of our imaginations. Its visual statements are abstract and theoretical.

Glass-and-steel modernism has undergone development. Many variations can be found in cities throughout the world and in the office parks dotting the American landscape. Most of these buildings are far less appealing than the Seagram tower, but they are recognizable as part of the modernist tradition in architecture, whose purpose is to provide the West with a clean visual slate, vast expanses of faceless glass on which to write a new history for mankind. Seen in this light, the dominance of modernism in the second half of the twentieth century was perhaps inevitable.

Over time, modernism gave way to a more playful and eclectic postmodernism, at least among patrons seeking a cutting-edge look. Architectural postmodernism makes use of the past but in whimsical ways. In the 1980s, Philip Johnson put a "Chippendale" notch in the top of what was then known as the AT&T Building (550 Madison Avenue), an ironic use of the past echoing the methods of critique that unmask and deconstruct. That is why the term "postmodernism" ended up encompassing both this playful architectural style and Derrida's literary theory, along with other movements of radical critique. Just as the progressive literary professor exposes the textual devices by which patriarchy or heteronormativity is made to seem like a normal and natural feature of society, so the postmodern architect shows how the motifs of the classical, Gothic, and other traditions are decorative gestures that hide, disguise, and distract. They are not components of a unified aesthetic that arises out of a shared, harmonious way of life. A postmodern building says to the viewer, "Style is arbitrary—just like justice and truth."

Nowadays, admired buildings draw on biological forms. Frank Gehry specializes in this aesthetic, which reflects a postwar strategy of disenchantment, the method that "goes small" through analysis in terms of biological function. A Frank Gehry building is like a Gary Becker economics paper analyzing marriage or other cultural forms in terms of preference maximization. Gehry's organic idiom might evoke the skeleton of a prehistoric animal or the twisting double helix of our genetic code. In either case, the architecture says that we are just animals, another open-society trope of disenchantment.

Some of today's architecture is not playful at all but reflects an explicit ideology of negation. Daniel Libeskind's design for the Jewish Museum in Berlin seeks to disorient visitors. The building has been hailed as a fitting architectural contribution to the postwar effort to confront the Holocaust without easy, comforting narratives. Other architects pursue this strategy in the design of courthouses and other public buildings, deliberately producing inhospitable environments on the theory that political authority is always, in truth, a system of attack. The architects and patrons responsible for these projects do not see themselves as anti-political or nihilistic. On the contrary, they believe that disorientation and negation—the weakening of Being—should be at the center of civic life. What may seem weird or even ugly to ordinary people is a salutary antiauthoritarian pedagogy.

By and large, the architecture of the West after World War II has followed Popper's prescription. The buildings that dominate our cities reflect a consensus about what almost destroyed the West—the closed society—and what is required for a better future—the open society. In its different aspects, postwar architecture seeks to prevent citizens from focusing their loyalties and uniting around coherent public symbols or historical traditions. The modernist aesthetic has put aside the "habit of deference" to the past, as Popper put it. Postmodernism, whether playfully or ponderously deconstructive, announces an aesthetic "nominalism," in which old styles and idioms are arbitrary and detachable. The architectural past is no more worthy of pious cultivation than are the metaphysical traditions that Popper deemed threats to the open society. Rough concrete and biological forms express the reductive, science-based approach to public life. They keep the strong gods at bay.

The social science Popper commends can reveal important truths, and architectural modernism and postmodernism are capable of a kind of beauty—austerely elegant or arrestingly exciting. The raw materials featured in modern architecture can awaken and enrich our aesthetic awareness, just as the spontaneous market forces that Hayek championed can produce wealth. There's no need to adopt a reactionary view. But we need to appreciate the cultural project of modern and postmodern architecture, which follows the postwar consensus. Our built environment since 1945 does not tell us a story about where we have come from and who we are. It inculcates a negative piety, urging us to affirm Vattimo's "destiny of weakening," which is why it can be international. The skyline of Frankfurt is indistinguishable from that of Minneapolis, which in turn looks a lot like Tokyo's. The architecture of the open society is borderless. It is an architecture of "lightening," unburdened by history and very nearly weightless, expressing reductive mathematical and biological truths. It follows John Rawls's prescription of keeping comprehensive doctrines out of the public landscape.

I could retell this story of weakening and lightening in other ways. Imagine a college freshman. He arrives with an inchoate but genuine enthusiasm for Henry James. He signs up for a course that features his novels. More likely than not, the course will focus on "critical reading." The young man will be taught to read James through the lens of class and feminism. Perhaps if he is bright he will get the hang of today's academic version of the postwar consensus. In his final paper he will show how James disrupts binary relationships between males and females by inserting a third figure, an "other" who "de-centers" the love drama. The essay is sure to earn him praise from his professor and encouragement to pursue further study. This pedagogy—paradigmatic for our late phase of the postwar era—replaces the student's warm love of James with a cooler expertise in critique. He may become more academically sophisticated, but his devotion to Henry James will be weakened, refocused on the patterns of power and injustice that his work exemplifies rather than the truth and beauty it embodies.

But enough—the pathways of disenchantment are countless. There is not a single elite-certified political, cultural, or intellectual trend that does not move in the direction of weakening. But we don't want to live this way. The personal choices of the rich and powerful people in the West (including not a few high-flying architects) indicate as much. They often prefer traditional architecture for their private homes. This is natural. We seek quietude in our domestic environment: serenity, stability, security, and repose. We want refuge from the ruthless competition of the marketplace. We seek relief from the shrill and sometimes brutal polemics of political life. We want a continuity that caresses us with what is familiar and inspires us with what is noble in our past.

The soccer coach yells at the goalkeeper who wanders too far up field, "Stay home!" His role is to protect the team's goal from attack. Traditional architecture can function like a goalkeeper. Amid today's relentless flux and change, its historical idioms establish continuity. Its familiar forms, anchored in generations of development and refinement, tell us we are part of something greater, something enduring and worthy of admiration. In a private house, these architectural forms reinforce the domestic sources of quietude: family history and marital fidelity. These are the great bulwarks against flux, change, and dissolution that make a house into a home rather than merely a residence.

The West is reaching a dead end because our leadership class, socialized into and loyal to the postwar consensus, insists that we must be homeless—even as it shelters itself. This is more than a matter of architectural styles. In the open society, we are instructed not to settle into stable convictions or common loves. Derrida described this unsettled condition as "play," a seemingly positive image. But we don't want to endlessly unpack, unmask, and undermine. Perhaps the current president of Harvard finds postmodern buildings off-putting and thinks today's literature professors are gadflies at best, intellectual shysters at worst. But he takes the larger view: They're good for society, contributing to the ongoing effort to promote openness and forestall the return of the strong gods.

The same acquiescence for the sake of openness is found at every level of the culture. Most education professionals think it's good for young children to have transgender teachers. Their opinion runs counter to common sense, which tells us that children need the stability that comes from being conformed to human reality, at the heart of which is the dichotomy between male and female. But the postwar consensus overrides common sense, celebrating the transgression that breaks down walls and inculcates the critical virtues necessary for sustaining an open society.

This is our crisis: a disquietude born of homelessness. I see it everywhere, the existential consequence of wholesale weakening. I'm shocked when I talk to the talented but anxious young people who have graduated from prominent universities. They distrust the system, even though the dynamic economy rewards their talents handsomely. But openness today means an intensely competitive marketplace for wealth and status without the guardrails and road maps of cultural norms. Feeling as though they are forever climbing a steep precipice without a safety rope, they find no stability, no rest—no home.

One conversation stands out. A younger friend, agonizing over the choices he faced in life, asked for advice. I told him I couldn't help very much. For me, life has been like a train ride. The engine of strong cultural norms pulled me through life's stages: college, job, marriage, children. In its time, the train will take me to retirement and, of course, death. He replied, "No, no—life's not like that anymore. Now it's a sailboat that you pilot first this way and then that in order to make your way to the destination of your own choosing." It struck me as an exhausting way to live.

Of course, nobody wants to live that way. For all their talk of an open economy and open society, those in the upper echelons of our society work very hard to protect their children. They carefully choose homes in neighborhoods with good schools, not trusting the open competition of merit, but instead giving their kids every advantage. They may join in the chorus that condemns traditional norms as authoritarian, but they keep their marriages together, and their families look like traditional ones. In other words, they share the basic human desire to protect one's children, to secure one's patrimony, to sustain and transmit a living inheritance. They shelter themselves and those whom they love—a natural and healthy impulse. The problem is that what our most powerful and capable fellow citizens do in private is at odds with what they insist upon in public.

I can't begin to account for all the sources of our disquietude, any more than I can unpack my friend's image of the self-piloted sailboat tacking one way and then another. I can only outline some themes and trends. These have been treated by others in greater detail. The effects of globalization on middle-class income have been widely discussed and debated. In his account of the meritocratic machine of elite education, *Excellent Sheep: The Miseducation of the American Elite and the Way to a Meaningful Life*, William Deresiewicz illuminates the reasons why my talented young friends so often feel at risk, even as they march from success to success. Peter Wood wrote the book on diversity—*Diversity: The Invention of a Concept*. Christopher Caldwell (*Reflections on the Revolution in Europe: Immigration, Islam, and the West*) and Douglas Murray (*The Strange Death of Europe: Immigration, Identity, Islam*) tell us more about the postwar politics of immigration than I can begin to summarize.

What I can add, however, is a thematic reframing what most of us know in terms of the metaphysical dreams of openness that now predominate. A great deal of the discussion and debate that goes under the rubric of populism reflects problems the postwar consensus either caused or is unable to address. Economic globalization, diversity ideology, and mass immigration enjoy the prestige of weakening and lightening. These powerful cultural imperatives explain why today's populism generates such anxiety among our leadership class, even to the point of hysterical worries about the return of the 1930s. Populism is more than a rebellion against outsourcing, political correctness, and too many foreigners. It is a rejection of the postwar consensus. This frightens our leadership class, for it has been socialized into the ahistorical conviction that the imperatives of the open society are the only legitimate basis for economic and political arrangements. All other alternatives, our establishment believes, lead back to fascism. They are roads to serfdom.

Understanding populism in light of the postwar consensus puts our present anxieties into perspective. Some say that homelessness is an intrinsic feature of modernity. Science disenchants the world and offers no supernatural consolations. Others say homelessness and disquietude are the inevitable price of technological progress and free markets. Still others blame liberalism. All true, perhaps. In any event, disquietude is as ancient as the fall of man. Cast out of Eden, we are always homeless. But the perennial uprootedness of the human condition—and the homelessness intensified by modernity—was so overemphasized by Popper and Hayek that it is now celebrated at the expense of anything strong and home-making. The openness we inherited from the postwar generation is no longer counterbalanced by consolidation and rootedness. We are afflicted by a domineering and obligatory openness.

When the transgression of Adam and Eve exposes them in their nakedness, God clothes them with what the Bible calls, enigmatically, "garments of skins." Something like this occurs in human history. We protect and cover when we build homes. We do this in the literal sense of erecting residences, and we do it when we enter into our cultural and spiritual traditions. The baseball player is at home on the diamond. The actor is at home in the spotlight. Everyone seeks to find places where he belongs. The essential task of political leadership is to help men shelter together within traditions and communities of shared loves. Unless we are clothed in this way, we are naked before the world.

The postwar consensus disrupts this necessary home-making. As I hope to show, the imperative of ever-greater openness has unbalanced the West. Our openness is the distorted mirror of the singular, untempered, and destructive passions and ideological fevers that shipwrecked the West in the first half of the twentieth century; it is their ideological opposite. And it is just as dangerous. A powerful vacuum and a powerful magnet both tear at the delicate fabric of life. If we can see the lack of balance in the imperatives of the open society, we can recognize that the populism currently challenging the political establishments of the West is not anti-modern, anti–free market, or anti-liberal. It rebels against the decadent dogmatism of the postwar consensus. That consensus, in turn, is not the end-of-history fulfillment of modern or liberal ideals but arose in particular historical circumstances as a profoundly one-sided response to the disasters that struck the West between 1914 and 1945.

## An Economy without Shelter

In the late 1940s, when Arthur Schlesinger Jr. wrote *The Vital Center: The Politics of Freedom*, the United States was unwinding its command-and-control wartime economy. Voters still haunted by the Great Depression prized the security of national solidarity, which had been reinforced by the war effort. Schlesinger did not discount this commitment. He recognized the dangers of openness without countervailing forces of consolidation and unity. Capitalism and technology disrupt traditional forms of community, often leaving individuals isolated. In such circumstances, as he and many other mainstream liberals recognized, communism's promise to restore solidarity could be dangerously alluring. American liberalism, Schlesinger argued, needed to pursue an anti-utopian, pragmatic approach to economic management, balancing individual initiative with collective responsibility—the economic equivalent of the educational balance between tradition and experimentation proposed by the Harvard committee, on which his father served.

Schlesinger's formula—markets moderated by government intervention and backstopped by social programs—has been the basis of America's center-left program throughout the postwar era. Likewise in Europe, despite the different political configurations after 1945, a balance between market dynamism and government-insured security was the goal. In recent decades, however, this balance has given way to an emphasis on economic openness, which is undoubtedly a source of today's populism.

In the early 1950s, the American economy was dominated by large companies working in concert with government agencies. Labor strife required government intervention, even to the point of Harry Truman's attempted nationalization of the steel industry in 1952. While the financial system continued to be regulated in accord with Depression-era legislation, free-market proponents like Milton Friedman urged greater economic openness and freedom, and the American people eventually tilted in that direction. President Jimmy Carter initiated the deregulatory agenda in the late 1970s, and it was realized to a large degree under Ronald Reagan in the 1980s.

The true power of a political consensus is seen when the debate ends and the opposition party signals its acquiescence. By the 1990s, Bill Clinton was announcing, "The era of big government is over." The center-left Democrats whom he led made their peace with economic deregulation. They reframed their historical commitment to labor as a promise that they would pursue economic openness with greater sensitivity to the needs of workers than would Republicans, whom they portrayed as captive to corporate interests.

By the late twentieth century, the bipartisan commitment to the open economy was obvious. The entire political establishment, left and right, in Europe and the United States, endorsed the expansion of global capital markets and the promotion of free trade. After the fall of the Berlin Wall, former Soviet satellites adopted free-market principles to a greater or lesser degree, while Russia itself underwent a "Big Bang" designed to jump-start a free economy in accord with Anglo-American principles. The agenda of economic liberalization gained support in Germany and elsewhere in Western Europe. In 1993, the European Economic Community became the European Union, allowing for more transnational economic activity, including the free movement of labor, goods, and capital. The General Agreement on Tariffs and Trade, established in 1947, was superseded by the World Trade Organization in 1994. Financial markets became vastly more extensive and liquid under the reign of the so-called Washington consensus.

All political projects involve compromise, and market liberalization is no exception. Domestic economies in the West remain heavily regulated, and there is still plenty of protectionism embedded in the global system. But Hayek's general principle came to be widely accepted: The more open markets are, the better life will be for everyone. The open global economy will lift up the poor, strengthen the economies of the West, and apply pressure to liberalize on closed societies such as China. So the postwar consensus promised, and so much of our leadership class still insists.

The political problem is obvious. The promises of economic openness have become less and less plausible in recent years. In *Global Inequality: A New Approach for the Age of Globalization*, Branko Milanovic demonstrates that while global economic liberalization has dramatically increased wealth overall, the new wealth has been allocated unevenly, especially in the West. This inequality has strained the social contract to the point of breaking.

Milanovic draws attention to an "elephant chart," so called because the curve is shaped like the body of an elephant, the far right side rapidly falling and then rapidly rising like an elephant's trunk.[1] This graph shows income growth in relation to income levels since the end of the Cold War. The elephant's large body begins with the tail touching the ground. This is the poorest part of the world, where income over the last thirty years has been stagnant. Quickly, however, income growth rises, outlining the great bulk of the elephant. This represents the rapidly growing economies of India and China and other Asian countries. In absolute terms, they remain poorer than the rich West (and Japan), but their middle-class incomes have grown rapidly, which is why the elephant's body looms so large. Now, however, we get to the trunk. In places like the United States, middle-class wages have been stagnant, and so the graph plunges, only to rise rapidly when we get to the winners in the global economy. This select cohort includes Saudi sheikhs and Chinese billionaires, but the majority of the winners are the wealthy denizens of the West who are plugged into the global economy. This is our leadership class.

Much of the story told by the elephant graph is well known. The remarkable growth in formerly impoverished countries stands as one of the great benefits of the end of the Cold War and the subsequent expansion of free markets throughout the world. We've also heard a great deal about income inequality in the United States and other Western countries, which is commonly identified as the source of political discontent and populism. In his study of economic history, *Capital in the Twenty-First Century*, Thomas Piketty comes to the gloomy conclusion that the trend toward greater economic inequality is intrinsic to the free-market system. This is the sort of assertion I prefer to leave to the economic theorists to debate.

What's less controversial is the stark fact of middle-class economic stagnation in the West. Specialists argue about the data. Some say that when one factors in lower costs for consumer goods and government transfer payments the stagnation is not so evident. Nevertheless, I will venture a broad judgment of our present circumstances: The erosion of the prosperity of the middle class in the West has undermined political solidarity. The prospects for moderately educated, middle-of-America workers have declined over the last generation, while globalization has worked out nicely for the well-educated, largely coastal elites. The specifics vary in other countries in the West, but the basic pattern is similar. The rich have a role in the global system; the middle class is increasingly homeless.

Postwar democratic legitimacy and political stability were based on the deep conviction among the members of the large middle class that their interests were in accord with those of the ruling class. Conflicts between labor and capital moderated after 1945 as the economic system provided stable, relatively lucrative roles for everyone from high school–educated workers to college graduates. Perhaps this was never really the case and the Marxist critics continued to have a point. But that's not important. Legitimacy and stability in public life depend upon perceptions as much as realities. You don't need a Ph.D. in political science to see that perceptions have changed in recent years. Middle-class voters throughout the West now worry that they will have no role in the globalized economy. They fear that their places will be taken by lower-cost workers abroad—if they haven't been taken already. This economic insecurity, a disquietude born of a system that tilts entirely in the direction of openness rather than solidarity, undoubtedly underlies the political turbulence of recent years.

We should have seen it coming. The members of the globalized leadership class in the West have made it clear over the past two decades that they don't need their fellow citizens of middling talent. In an analysis in 2012 of the shift in technology manufacturing from the United States to China, reporters for the *New York Times* found that nearly all of Apple's products were manufactured abroad. "It isn't just that workers are cheaper abroad," the journalist noted. "Rather, Apple's executives believe the vast scale of overseas factories as well as the flexibility, diligence and industrial skills of foreign workers so outpaced their American counterparts that 'Made in America' is no longer a viable option for most Apple products."[2]

It is worth pausing over this formulation of competitive advantage. What does it really mean to say that manufacturing high-tech products in the United States is "no longer a viable option"? The problem is not the "vast scale." Apple and other large companies could easily afford capital investments in large plants in the United States. In the eyes of our corporate leaders, it is the American worker who is no longer "viable." Over the past three decades we have heard endless praise of the "creative class," the highly talented, well-educated Americans who can "add value," as the consultants put it. Median-talented Americans? There is no role for them. Apparently, they are too inflexible, lack diligence, and are unskilled. In a dynamic global economy, they are deadweight—"closed," not "open."

These are not the sentiments of cigar-smoking robber barons who own coal mines in West Virginia. They're expressed by T-shirt-wearing tech executives who are pillars of the center-left establishment in the United States. Nor are these rich and powerful people saying that China produces extraordinarily fine and creative software engineers. When it comes to top talent, the ruling class in the West believes in itself. It regularly champions the universities it graduated from as "the best in the world," making record donations to their already gigantic endowments.

For thirty years, as globalization has gathered momentum, journalists, academics, business leaders, and politicians have hailed America as uniquely capable of inculcating entrepreneurial drive and encouraging creative innovation. They are interested in the successful people, those who are on the rising trunk of Milanovic's elephant chart. Steve Jobs, Jeff Bezos, Larry Ellison—*they* are the flower of our society, the crucial sources of our prosperity. We owe them our gratitude! The ordinary people? That's another story. They are too complacent, not willing to retrain and relocate—"takers" with lousy work habits, losers who can't pass a drug test. Few are so blunt, but this opinion is implicit in a great deal of commentary on economic globalization over the past two decades.

Since the election of Donald Trump, the American leadership class is more circumspect in its public pronouncements. Nevertheless, its rhetorical signals remain strong, and its actions tell a consistent story. The movement of capital abroad indicates that many corporate leaders believe that Asian workers are better partners for the future than the middle class in the West. This abandonment of ordinary workers marks how far along the trajectory of postwar openness we have come. These days, "progressives" update Arthur Schlesinger's vision of economic freedom balanced by government-provided security with calls for "guaranteed basic income." This redistributive plan gives money to those in the West who have no place in the global economy. Such a policy proposal makes an important statement about solidarity. Our center-left leadership class will promise to subsidize working-class consumption, but it won't reorient the global economy toward their employment. It all but explicitly announces that many people in the West have no place in the open economy of the future. Future elites and their children will have roles, of course—crucial and remunerative roles as "innovators." They will be sheltered quite nicely.

American liberalism, once the patron of the "forgotten man," has come a long way from the economic solidarity that 1950s liberals like Arthur Schlesinger envisioned.

## The Open Culture

In the first decade after 1945, American conservatism took a different approach to achieving a balance from the one Schlesinger outlined. Robert Taft—"Mr. Republican," the most prominent spokesman for conservatism in the early 1950s—ardently opposed the intrusive economic policies of the Roosevelt era, but economic freedom was not his only priority. He, too, endorsed countervailing, sheltering forces. As he once put it, "Before our system can claim success, it must not only create a people with a higher standard of living, but a people with a higher standard of character—character that must include religious faith, morality, educated intelligence, self-restraint, and an ingrained demand for justice and unselfishness."[3]

Instead of depending on government regulation and programs—the center-left approach—the postwar center-right proposed a strong moral and religious culture as the source of the continuity, stability, and solidarity that allow citizens to feel at home amid the dynamism of a free economy. William F. Buckley struck a similar balance in *God and Man at Yale* when he paired an ardent defense of economic individualism with equally ardent pleas for patriotism and the restoration of Christian faith. This is the agenda that the American right followed for decades.

In theory, 1950s liberals supported the "higher standard of character" that Taft and other Republicans emphasized. But in practice, establishment liberals were already ambivalent, as the violent reactions to Walter Lippmann's book in the mid-1950s indicate. They worried about the "authoritarian" implications of strong moral claims, preferring softer notions of "meaning" and a public philosophy based on the facts of social science. The anti-anticommunist stance of highbrow liberals was another sign of center-left ambivalence about the role of strong cultural authority in an open society. As James Burnham lamented in *Suicide of the West*, by the early 1960s, American liberals often echoed anti-Western sentiments, wallowing in an enervating self-criticism rather than cheering the achievements of the West. Their rhetoric was one of weakening, not strengthening.

The movement toward cultural openness on the left was inevitable, it seems. Even in the 1950s, the meaning of "progressive" was beginning to shift, the economic emphasis—favoring labor over capital—giving way to cultural concerns that favored openness. Progressives fought against racial injustice. Soon they supported women's liberation and the sexual revolution. And though some resisted, under elite leadership public sentiment moved in the direction of openness and cultural deregulation. On its fringes, the political left became anti-American, regarding ardent patriotism as retrograde and reactionary—an engine of the authoritarian personality and a sign of crypto-fascism. George McGovern's disastrous presidential campaign was captive to the "weakening of Being" that took hold of the Democratic Party in 1972, and in a triumph of the consolidating theme of "law and order" over "flower power," Richard Nixon coasted to a landslide victory.

But this conservative victory was temporary. The prestige of openness grew with time, eroding the moral and religious authority that Taft positioned as the counterbalance to economic openness. Just as the center-left reconciled itself to the postwar emphasis on openness in the economy, the center-right made its peace with ever greater cultural openness. The emergence of the religious right as a political force masked this capitulation for a while, but by the twenty-first century the establishment center-right's embrace of cultural deregulation was as complete as the establishment center-left's affirmation of economic deregulation.

This story can be told as the ascendancy of libertarianism as the house philosophy of the Republican Party, but it is more accurately described as the triumph of the principle of diversity. Unlike libertarian philosophy, rooted in nineteenth-century Anglo-American liberalism, diversity makes sense only within the postwar consensus, with its fusion of the imperatives of an open economy and an open culture. The concept came to prominence after the Supreme Court invoked it in *Regents of the University of California v. Bakke* (1978). Justice Lewis Powell's plurality opinion declared a "diverse student body" a legitimate goal for an educational institution because it enhances the learning environment, improving conditions for "speculation, experiment and creation."

Powell drew the diversity argument from a brief submitted by some of the Ivy League universities. It was obvious at the time that the real issue was racial justice, not "diversity." Concerned to protect their affirmative action admissions policies, the elite institutions worried that if giving preference to black applicants was declared unconstitutional, their student bodies would become nearly all white once again, a scandalous retreat from the gains of the civil rights movement.

In the 1970s, America's leadership class was trying to find its footing. On their face, the laws against discrimination passed in the early 1960s stipulated that all persons must be treated equally with respect to race. That mandate of justice, which is a strong god, requires race-blind policies, not the race-conscious policies with which universities recruited black students. To avoid that mandate, our leadership class turned to the muddy concept of "diversity," championing its purported benefits.

It was Popper's "social technologists" who made "diversity" a fig leaf for policies they thought were necessary for overcoming the legacy of racial discrimination. They imagined it a temporary measure that would prepare the way for the eventual return of the strong god of color-blind justice. Very quickly, however, diversity became a good to be pursued for its own sake. In the 1980s, Harold Shapiro, then president of the University of Michigan, outlined an expansive vision of diversity. The proper mix of race, sex, ethnicity, and religion, he promised, would contribute to "freedom of thought, innovation, and creativity." Sexual orientation and other categories were soon added to the list, and corporations joined universities on the diversity bandwagon, asserting that a diverse workforce was essential for business success.

There is no evidence that any of this is true. One of the bastions of corporate diversity-talk, Silicon Valley, combines leadership in technology with some of the most racially homogeneous communities in California. Moreover, "diversity" is hopelessly ill-defined. Diversity with respect to what? But these and other liabilities are of no moment. The rhetoric of diversity took hold because it evokes openness and expresses the ideals and aspirations of the postwar consensus. By the end of the twentieth century, the title "diversity officer" supplanted "affirmative action officer" in human resource departments, a sign that the imperatives of openness had sidelined those of justice.

In retrospect, diversity's replacement of racial justice as the civil rights ideal was foreordained. In its classic phase, the civil rights movement appealed to the justice due to every man, regardless of the color of his skin, a standard that limits what can and cannot be done. Diversity does something different. It promises to promote open-mindedness and a more expansive outlook, a benefit for everyone. "Diversity training" is sold as a way to put an end to *all* forms of discrimination and exclusion while promoting an environment in which everyone is welcome and everyone has a role—a home without walls.

By the twenty-first century, diversity had become in many circles an omnibus term for America's highest ideals. In his 2016 State of the Union speech, Barack Obama told the American public, "The world respects us not just for our arsenal, it respects us for our diversity and our openness." A failure to "include" is not only a sin against justice but also a violation of the sacred ideal of diversity. As Obama put it, "It betrays who we are as a country."

What this means in reality can be hard to pin down. Does our failure to admit everyone in the world who wants to immigrate to the United States "betray who we are"? Are borders contrary to the American ideal? Closer to home, as any conservative university student knows, the commitment to a "diverse student body," so often reiterated by educators, does not mean a diversity of political views. But the vagueness and apparent contradictions don't matter. Diversity is a slogan of the open society. It isn't a principle. It's a therapy. One does not learn about diversity; one is trained in it.

The related concept of multiculturalism is subject to similar vagueness and apparent contradictions. How can it critique and censure Western culture while celebrating non-Western cultures? Is censuring Saudi Arabia for prohibiting Christian worship contrary to the tenets of multiculturalism? Anyone who imagines that such questions matter mistakes multiculturalism for a principled outlook. Like diversity, it is another post-1945 open-society therapy. Multiculturalism focuses on disenchanting the Western tradition because it alone has a hold on our spiritual and political imagination and provides us with a home. So, for example, progressives in Europe attack strong expressions of Christianity but accommodate rigid and illiberal forms of Islam. They do this because Christianity is a strong god of the West whose return must be prevented. Islam is not, and so need not be feared—or so they imagine. The logic of multiculturalism, therefore, is paradoxically Eurocentric. It exists only to address our particularly Western nightmares of concentration camps and lynchings.

The regime of diversity and multiculturalism seeks to make boundaries open, porous, and fluid. Moral judgments should be personal and open-ended. Anyone or anything animated by strong gods is by definition "opposed to diversity." This is the same logic by which Walter Lippmann was condemned as a crypto-fascist even though his purpose in writing *Essays in the Public Philosophy* was to strengthen the foundations of our liberal culture. His crime was to want to consolidate, not deconsolidate, to strengthen, not weaken. In the eyes of those imbued with the postwar consensus, this made him the enemy of an open society. Today, someone who speaks in favor of marriage is denounced as "heteronormative" and a crypto-racist. Someone who urges a renewal of patriotism is condemned for his supposed nostalgia for an "all-white 1950s." If we seek to reestablish a metaphysical basis for human rights, or ground them in natural law, LGBT activists immediately sense a threat and recast these efforts as homophobic. They are in a sense right. Anything that encourages the strengthening of Being is opposed to diversity, which requires breaking down boundaries and deregulating culture.

The public exaltation of diversity in recent years corresponds to the hardening of the postwar consensus into dogma. It has tightened its hold on the center-right as well as the center-left. At the same time that curriculum committees and education professionals began to champion diversity, business journals started to emphasize it as well, extolling its promise of innovation and creativity. In these early decades of the twenty-first century, establishment Republicans sing the praises of diversity with as much gusto as liberals.

This has been coming for a long time. When he ran for reelection in 1992, President George H. W. Bush, speaking to a group of evangelical leaders in Dallas, Texas, echoed the old Taft theme, updated for the era in which the religious right had become a powerful political force. He told the churchmen that Democrats must be defeated because their party platform left out "three simple letters, G-O-D." But his heart wasn't in it. He disliked pandering to old-line voters who still wanted blunt, strong assurances that their country was anchored in religious and moral truths. His son George W. Bush, whose Christian conviction was perhaps more demotic, sought something like Bill Clinton's modus vivendi with the postwar consensus. The notion of "compassionate conservatism" was meant to signal a softening and weakening of older assertions of moral and religious authority. Nobody ever declared, "The era of the Moral Majority is over," at least not in so many words. But the analysis of Mitt Romney's loss to Barack Obama in 2012 commissioned by the Republican National Committee urged a more "multicultural" party, which amounted to the same thing.

Like economic openness, which has been retailed as good for everyone, cultural openness and deregulation are billed as purely beneficial. Diversity will bring racial justice and end discrimination; it will promote critical thinking and innovation; it will open our imaginations and broaden our experiences; it will make us happier; it will make us wealthier because we will be more creative and more adaptable to the global marketplace. Cultural openness and deregulation are a win-win proposition, we are told. There is no downside.

Many are losing confidence in the promises of economic openness, and the promises of cultural openness are becoming harder to believe as well. In his important book *Coming Apart: The State of White America, 1960–2010*, Charles Murray documents the trend toward dysfunction on the lower rungs of society. Well-to-do Americans have handled fifty years of openness reasonably well, but cultural deregulation has been hell on the bottom 30 percent. Many people took issue with Donald Trump's dark inaugural address in January 2017, with its talk of "carnage." "Aren't things pretty good?" they asked. That response is evidence for Murray's thesis that over the past two generations there has been a pronounced divergence in quality of life between the open society's winners and losers. The upper portion of society has an economic and cultural home in the system; those at the bottom do not. Meanwhile, denizens of the vulnerable middle class are anxious that they, too, will be homeless, sidelined in the global economy and lumped among the "uncreative" and close-minded. The upper end of society is sheltered, the rest are not.

The virtue of solidarity—the sense of fraternity and common destiny among all members of a society—is based on shared convictions and loyalties, which are consolidating and unifying, not "diversifying." President Barack Obama often tried to square the circle by declaring that diversity itself is a shared, unifying value—open minds are our great strength, and so forth—and countless university presidents have made the same assertion, but it yields an unstable pseudo-solidarity. To a certain degree, we can unify around diversity and other motifs of openness, as we have done for a number of decades. But a commitment to ever-greater dispersion, difference, and openness atomizes rather than consolidates, stripping us naked rather than clothing us.

The trajectory is plain to see. The more our leadership class has championed diversity and multiculturalism, the more powerful identity politics has become. Those who gravitate toward "identity" have the correct intuition that solidarity requires a shared loyalty. Because the relentless pursuit of the open-society agenda deprives them of a strong civic identity, they fall back on race, sex, sexual orientation, or some other "identity," a process that reinforces and is reinforced by the postwar consensus. Identity politics accentuates the differences that diversity and other therapies of openness promote and redirects our desire for solidarity by focusing it on DNA (race and sex) and sexual practices. These are open-society tropes as well. Identity politics constructs a pseudo-politics that depends on grievance and moral outrage, preventing citizens from consolidating around shared civic projects—other than affirming the open society as an end in itself.

Recent polling shows that young people believe racial discrimination is worse now than it was in the past—a ridiculous misapprehension stoked by the therapy of diversity and the rhetoric of multiculturalism, which make differences more consequential, visible, and fraught. This, in turn, breeds anxiety about belonging and having a home, and that anxiety calls for still more diversity training and greater and more minute "recognition of difference," as if this pseudo-politics could somehow produce a new, inclusive, borderless, and "open" solidarity, a home without walls.

Our situation today is not a happy one. Cultural deregulation was always implicit in the early postwar campaign against the "authoritarian personality" and in the shift from truth to meaning. It has become explicit in diversity therapies and multicultural rhetoric. The open society can tolerate no strong cultural norms, for they define the domain of the "normal." Recent dustups over the supposedly racist implications of advocating marriage, thrift, and a good work ethic reveal the logic of cultural deregulation. The goal is to strip society of norms, leaving unsheltered those who cannot afford to live in well-appointed enclaves that covertly sustain modified bourgeois norms for the rich and their children. In the open culture, the lives of ordinary people become more disordered and less functional. Civic solidarity is undermined and fears about discrimination fester. When racial tensions increased during Obama's eight years as president, commentators assumed the cause was white backlash. This is always the pattern of the postwar consensus: social problems stem from closed-society vices. Our leadership class is unable to countenance the obvious explanation: *They are dysfunctions of an open society.*

The loss of solidarity and the degradation of living conditions among the poor and middle class would be bad enough, but there's more. The decadent postwar consensus encourages contempt by the few for the many. To a remarkable extent, our leadership class derides and dismisses those whom it leads, fueling the explosive antiestablishment resentment that characterizes today's populism.

Derrida was prescient. He saw that the privileged "center" needs to be broken down to open things up. That's what the method of deconstruction does with texts. We've done the same thing in culture. In the 1950s and 1960s, the ideal employee for a major corporation was a married man. His domestic responsibilities were thought to make him steady and reliable. By 2000, the dominant cultural ideals had shifted toward fluidity and openness, epitomized in the notion of diversity. Now, the cherished employee is single, perhaps gay, but certainly eccentric to the mainstream and thus more likely to be innovative, creative, and mobile. The stolid middle-class person who is married, goes to church, and has a network of communal responsibilities has become a liability in the open economy and open culture. He's the sort of person who is "inflexible." He's likely to be "conventional." What's needed, says the postwar consensus at this late stage, are nimble, self-creating personalities able to boldly test the boundaries. The media are fixated on transgendered celebrities, multicultural settings, and other "de-centering" stories and images. This trend is not the result of conscious propaganda but reflects heartfelt efforts to "do the right thing" by promoting more diverse and inclusive images. This, we believe, will build an open culture.

But building an open culture is not a bloodless project. It involves redeploying cultural power. When Derrida speaks of de-centering, he is only talking about texts. When Vattimo commends the weakening of Being, he limits himself to abstractions. But "de-centering" means driving what was once privileged to the margins, and in real life that is accomplished through shaming, mocking, and deriding— a tactic otherwise known as "political correctness." In *The Authoritarian Personality*, the researchers used "fascist" as a shaming word, applying it to people of traditional religious or moral views. We do the same thing with diversity and those who "lack" it, though we disguise the punitive shaming with the win-win rhetoric that promises a place for everyone in the open culture.

Barack Obama famously dismissed those who were insufficiently appreciative of his leadership as "clinging to their guns and religion"—a remark that exposed, perhaps, the hauteur of an Ivy League high-achiever more than anything else. But that's the point. Diversity—embodying it, appreciating it, championing it—establishes one's high social status and provides a weapon for attacking the low-status people who supposedly lack it. After Britain's vote to leave the European Union, countless commentators fell unselfconsciously into derogating those who voted for "Brexit" as rustics, rubes, and racists while implicitly complimenting themselves as cosmopolitan and inclusive. Something similar has been at work in the United States for some time. You can "have" diversity even if you live in a gated community simply by mouthing the pieties of the open culture. Those who don't are, as Hillary Clinton notori- ously put it, "deplorables."

A national politician is always ill-advised to attack very nearly half the country. But for those in the grip of the postwar consensus, the impulse to do so is irresistible. The imperative of openness shifts moral prestige away from the "center" and toward the "periphery." Those who transgress, break down boundaries, and include the mar- ginalized are seen as exemplary citizens, even if they limit their trans- gression to words. They promote an open society. They serve the common good by weakening norms. Those who trumpet diversity, innovation, and transgression deserve to rule, not the "clingers" who are susceptible to "nostalgia" and vulnerable to "fear," if not outright racism. This is what the postwar consensus trains us to believe.

Conveniently enough, the university-educated, well-to-do Amer- icans who win in the open economy are the very same people who the open-society consensus tells us deserve to rule—the virtuous champions of diversity. As Darel Paul shows in his study of the polit- ical and cultural history of gay rights, *From Tolerance to Equality: How Elites Brought America to Same-Sex Marriage*, loyalty to the diversity agenda (in all its aspects and not just gay rights) correlates strongly with educational status and income. The upshot is a politi- cally toxic division of the West into two camps. In one we find the members of the "creative class," who are told (and tell themselves) that they both deserve financial rewards (innovation drives growth!) and have all the virtues necessary to build the anti-fascist, anti-racist, and open society that will redeem the West. In the other camp lan- guish the economic and cultural losers. They are the "takers" who also lack a proper zeal for diversity. They are the "angry white men" who voted for Brexit and Donald Trump, or so we are told.

Put simply, the open-culture side of the postwar consensus dove- tails with the open-economy side to reinforce the prestige and power of the leadership class. This power is not a matter of degree. It is absolute. They *must* rule; otherwise, we will backslide into stagnation (a closed economy) and oppression (a closed society). Without their leadership, the "takers," who just want "free stuff," will destroy our vibrant economy, and the racists, xenophobes, and fascists will force women back into subservience and reestablish white supremacy.

It is this all-or-nothing dogmatism, not populism, that threatens our political culture, for it justifies appeals to emergency measures to prevent any diminution of the power of the postwar consensus and the elites imbued with its moral prestige. Appeals to a state of emergency are now commonplace at universities, shutting down discussion and debate. When someone's "dignity" is harmed by politically incorrect views, university administrators use their police power to put an end to the "assault." Similar repression is likely to occur on a larger, even national, scale in Europe and America. It is not unimaginable that the European Court of Human Rights, in the not so distant future, will declare a Hungarian or Polish election invalid because the winner is insufficiently devoted to diversity or some other shibboleth of the open society. Such an election, by the logic of the postwar consensus, would violate human dignity. In the United States, the antidemocratic future of the postwar consensus is foreshadowed in the coalition of establishment Republicans and Democrats that has worked overtime to delegitimize the Trump presidency, by legal means or otherwise. These people are convinced that they are not partisans. Rather, they see themselves as guardians of the open society, saving us from authoritarianism, fascism, racism, or some other moral evil.

### Open Borders

Attacking lax immigration policies has been the most effective way for antiestablishment politicians and parties to win support. This makes sense. Open borders are an emblem of the open society. Immigration policy over the past few decades has exposed middle-class workers to wage competition and has disrupted settled patterns of cultural transmission. The preference for open borders among elites, often unspoken but almost always strongly felt, exposes their profound refusal to shelter those whom they lead.

In *The Strange Death of Europe: Immigration, Identity, Islam*, Douglas Murray recounts what is by now a familiar story. The nations of Europe are experiencing a profound demographic change. Since 1945, people from non-European lands have immigrated to the West in large numbers. Some have come in accord with government policies put in place decades ago to deal with labor shortages. Others are being settled as a result of emergency measures to accommodate refugees from the war-torn Middle East. Still others arrive illegally. Murray tells a complex story about religion, culture, and national identity, a story that is still unfolding. One strand, however, stands out as remarkably constant. For more than fifty years, voters in Europe have told their leaders that they don't like the cultural changes caused by immigration and they don't want more immigrants. The politicians consistently promise to reduce the inflow. But they never do.

In many instances, the leadership class pushes in the opposite direction, toward more immigration, while it celebrates "diversity" as redemptive. Over the past two generations, the political establishment of Europe has used its cultural power to censure and denounce as "racists" and "fascists" those who object to immigration. Murray tells the story of Ray Honeyford, a Yorkshire headmaster who in 1984 published an article about the failure of Muslim immigrant children to assimilate in his school. For making the obvious point that the then-nascent multicultural ideology discouraged assimilation, making the problem worse, he was denounced as a "Raycist" and drummed out of his job. A decade later, the Labor government minister responsible for immigration policy declared that calls for limitations on immigration were motivated by racism. The Conservative Party took power in the United Kingdom in 2010 with promises to cut immigration. Since that date immigration has risen.

As Murray's detailed account shows, European immigration policy has differed from country to country, but the power of the postwar consensus is evident everywhere. As economic openness has become a central imperative, a more or less explicit presumption in favor of open borders has followed as a matter of course. The European Union's internal policy of free movement of labor is a clear instance of this. The political backlash after the German chancellor Angela Merkel's decision to allow more than a million refugees to enter Europe in 2015 has led to sustained efforts to control migration. To some degree they have worked. But the postwar consensus views these efforts as an unfortunate concession to the limited horizons of ordinary people who are not yet "ready" for a truly open society.

The arguments for liberal immigration policies are many. In Europe and the United States, economists warn that social entitlements will be unsustainable without stepped-up immigration to sustain economic growth. Others argue that Europe's slumping birth rates would otherwise doom it to economic stagnation. In a different register, economists worry that the lack of low-wage immigrant labor will spark inflation. Versions of these arguments appear on the *Wall Street Journal* editorial page and elsewhere.

I don't want to assess the rationales for liberal immigration policies. It is sufficient to say that the arguments are legion. In every case they express one or another version of the win-win logic of the postwar consensus. Just as open global markets will make us all wealthier, eventually, so too will open labor markets, which allow people to flow toward economic opportunity. The win-win economic arguments are reinforced by the win-win promises of diversity and multiculturalism.

Old Europe will be revitalized by the fresh energy of new cultures. Opportunities for dialogue and mutual enrichment will arise, sparking creativity and innovation. And, of course, the food will be better. Just look at London, a multicultural city that has flourished in recent decades!

Lurking behind these cheerful claims are more somber thoughts, spawned by the memory of Auschwitz. Formed by the postwar consensus, the leadership class in the West sees its fundamental duty in historical terms: to prevent the return of the strong gods. Immigrants thus become important assets, not threats, as ordinary voters regard them. They bring diversity, which is the firewall against resurgent racism and fascism. A young Canadian law student writing recently against restrictions on migration worries about the "politics of demonization and fear." But she takes heart. There are good signs: "Counter movements have rallied together across nations in support of connectedness and inclusion." They have launched initiatives "aimed at creating intercultural understanding, facilitating open and inclusive dialogue, and challenging the current crisis of prejudice and exclusion." The title of her blog post was the signal cliché of the postwar consensus: "Diversity Is Our Strength."[4]

Experienced politicians are not likely to put the matter so simplistically. Nevertheless, this law student expresses the imperative widely shared among those who lead the West. They have in the back of their minds the dogmas of the postwar consensus. Unless we build an open society, we will backslide into the closed societies of the past. Some of them are gloomier, concluding that, after Auschwitz, the West does not deserve to endure. They welcome the mass migration that will fundamentally change the Western culture that produced so many decades of catastrophe. This change should be welcomed as a blessed deliverance from a cursed inheritance. These thoughts, often repressed, are no less powerful for being unacknowledged. The imperatives of the open society, not economic arguments about the benefits of immigration or even moral arguments about the West's duty to refugees, are the most powerful cause of the establishment leaders' reluctance to curtail immigration. The same imperatives explain why they denounce as racist and fascist the populist politicians who promise to do so.

## Leaders without Loyalty

During a debate in Europe about immigration, an impassioned speech by a young French woman opened my eyes to the fragility of the now decadent postwar consensus. She told her listeners that she was middle class and therefore could not afford to live in French-only neighborhoods that have no Muslim immigrants, as the rich French do. So she knows their ways, which include returning to Tunisia or Algeria during the holidays to visit relatives. They are explicit, she said, in how they describe these trips. They are cherished opportunities to "go home." Her voice then broke with emotion, and she asked, trembling, "If I lose France, where can I go?" The room was silent. We all felt the piercing anguish of her question, which we knew we could not answer.

I can think of no fear more politically explosive than that of homelessness. Our souls are profoundly unsettled when we contemplate being cast into the world naked and unprotected. This is why refugees inspire anguish. They are homeless. Taking the measure of the economic, cultural, and immigration policies of her own government, the young French woman glimpsed a terrifying possibility. Those whom she must trust to lead the West may well turn her into a refugee.

She trembled for good reason, not because of irrational phobias. The postwar consensus is stoking a political crisis. It consigns most people in the West to a condition of homelessness. This was always part of the logic of the open society. Popper asserted that the notion of national identity is based on "magical" thinking. Calls to preserve an English or a French culture amount to "anti-humanitarian pro-paganda." Of course, in the early decades of the postwar era, the proponents of an open society could take its underlying solidarity for granted. The Cold War kept the West tensed with collective pur-pose. But the demise of the Soviet Union removed limits to utopian ideals of openness, which now bear upon us with dissolving urgency.

Our leadership class is utterly out of balance. Prominent voices amplify Popper rather than mute him. They want to call the young French woman Islamophobic or racist, which is to say, "anti-human-itarian." Today, concerns about cultural continuity are almost always depicted as harbingers of resurgent racism, fascism, and—Auschwitz. In his denunciation of "collectivism," Hayek taught that notions such as national character or "destiny" lead to serfdom. "England for the English"—doesn't that spring from the same malign impulse that gave rise to Hitler's race-based fascism? And hasn't our critical edu-cation shown us that borders are artificial constructs and the nation-state a relatively recent invention? And aren't the populist calls for closed borders clear indications of a reactionary impulse, a neo-colonialist effort to cling to the privileges of the "center"? Don't we owe to those who "fear change" the pedagogy of "de-familiarization"? Isn't it the height of public service to make education in diversity obligatory for all?

Who hasn't heard expressions of these and other lines of thought? Socialized into the dogmas of the postwar consensus, our leadership class will enforce borders or renew solidarity only reluctantly and temporarily (though they will of course continue to shelter them-selves). When talking to a smart graduate student in Cambridge, Massachusetts, doing work in social policy, I was not surprised to discover that he could not formulate a reason to give preference to an unemployed worker in Ohio over someone in Senegal who wants to migrate to the United States. More and more voters in the West sense this strange inability among our leadership class to affirm their loyalty to the people they lead. And so voters suspect, correctly, that those who lead are not willing to protect them from economic competition or cultural displacement. Their leaders will not do what leaders are supposed to do, which is to protect and preserve the realm, to sustain and build up our shared home.

This suspicion is growing. It is driving antiestablishment politics, and it foretells a shift in the Western cultural consensus away from the weakening motifs that have predominated in recent decades. Today's populism rejects the deregulatory "openness" consensus. One of Trump's most striking campaign promises was to build a "beautiful wall" on our southern border, a symbol of closure, not openness. Trump attacked other aspects of the bipartisan establishment as well, promising to rip up free-trade agreements and to protect American industries. He repeatedly, pungently, and unapologetically violated the canons of political correctness, the police arm of cultural openness. And his entire campaign was based on an unnuanced, pro-American slogan: "Make America Great Again."

These signature stances sin against the postwar consensus. During the campaign, mainstream conservatives howled with indignation about the threat Trump posed to free-market principles. Foreign policy experts warned that he would torpedo the "rules-based international order." Liberals were outraged that Trump's (to them) obvious demonstrations of sexism, racism, and general hostility to every principle of an open and inclusive society failed to derail his candidacy. What's wrong with American voters?

One of Trump's major speeches added an exclamation point to his rejection of the postwar consensus. Poland was the scene of some of the most brutal episodes of the Second World War, one of which was the slaughter by the retreating Nazis of the Polish underground resistance in Warsaw in the summer of 1944, while the Red Army deliberately delayed its advance. We are trained to speak of this and other horrors as lessons about the dangers of totalitarianism, nativism, anti-Semitism, and other perversions, all of which call for the opposing virtues of the open society. But speaking in Warsaw in 2017, Trump instead praised the heroism of the Warsaw Uprising. For decades, political leaders in the West have been saying, "Never again." Trump said, "Let us all fight like the Poles—for family, for freedom, for country, and for God." The Polish inheritance, he said, was sanctified with the blood of sacrifice. (The reference to blood as the seal of a sacred fraternal bond was a shocking transgression of a postwar European taboo.) His praise of national reconsolidation was a call for the strengthening of Being, not its weakening.

Many of the responses to Trump's speech went entirely according to script. The liberal journalist Peter Beinart derided Trump's assertion that the fundamental question we face "is whether the West has the will to survive" as "a statement of racial and religious paranoia." Muslim immigrants, he wrote, "only threaten the West's 'survival' if by 'West' you mean white, Christian hegemony."[5] The *New York Times* described parts of the speech as "dark and confrontational," an acknowledgment that Trump seems to reject the win-win promises of openness. Jeva Lange thought the speech betrayed the true values of the West—openness and diversity. These responses, sincere though they may be, could have been written by computer bots programmed by the postwar consensus. Any talk of strengthening or consolidating solidarity is taken as a sign of resurgent racism and fascism, which must be countered by ever more ardent reaffirmations of weakening. This reaction discredits the postwar consensus, for it exposes its willingness to make us homeless.

Populism, which is unique to democratic modernity, is not a political philosophy. In a democratic system, a governing consensus ordinarily frames the back-and-forth of partisan electoral politics. At certain times, however, the consensus becomes decadent and dysfunctional. The *demos* becomes unsettled. Out of this restlessness populism arises, which is often undifferentiated and sometimes destructive. When the ruling class ignores or derides the unsettled populace ("deplorables," "takers," "racists," "Islamophobes," "fascists," and so forth), the restlessness jells into an adversarial mood. A populist gains political power on the strength of this adversarial stance. He opposes the governing consensus, attacking its political embodiment, the establishment.

By this definition, Trump is undoubtedly a populist, as are anti-establishment politicians in Europe. At one of his campaign rallies he said, "Our country is being run by very stupid people." As a description of native intelligence and expertise, this is implausible. But it resonated as an attack on the political establishment. It was, in truth, a generous attack. It encouraged voters to adopt the forgiving view that they were being betrayed out of incompetence, not deliberately by Western elites who would sell them out to the win-win promises of the open economy, open culture, and open borders—promises that in reality mean only they win.

Trump's message to voters was not "I will open things up to create opportunity and economic growth." It was "I will defend you." His message was not "Diversity is our strength." It was "America is for Americans." His message was not "Our job is to lead the world." It was "My job is to look out for our country's interests."

Think what you want of Trump, ill or well, but think clearly. He contradicts the postwar governing consensus, as do many populist political figures in Europe. He is the anti–George H. W. Bush: strong borders, not open ones; advantageous trade, not open trade; loyalty and patriotism, not open minds.

Our leadership class is not wrong to be nervous about what Trump and other populists represent. We have a great deal to lose. An open society can be wealthy and moderate. Technocratic rationality of the sort encouraged by Popper can lead to well-considered policies. Hayek and Friedman were correct. The decentered play of self-interest in the marketplace can generate wealth and give us elbow room to make up our own minds about how to live.

But the open society alone fails to meet our basic human need for a home. True solidarity is not close-minded complacency. It is an active loyalty that aspires to be faithful to a shared love. Trump praised this loyalty in the Polish patriots who rose up in Warsaw. Without loyalty and the solidarity it breeds we become disquieted, even amidst our pleasures, riches, and relative comity.

All flesh is like grass. Donald Trump will pass from the scene, as will the other politicians now in the news. But they foretell change, not just in what they say but in the often exaggerated, anxious, and hysterical responses they evoke from a failing establishment in the West. The rising tide of populism suggests a rejection of the postwar consensus. The winds are shifting. More and more people in the West want the strong gods to return.

## CHAPTER FIVE

# The Return of the Strong Gods

I n 1912, Émile Durkheim published a theory of the social function of religion, *The Elementary Forms of Religious Life*. As he recognized, formal religious practice and belief account for only part of our engagement with the sacred. Monotheism, Jewish and Christian, drove out the gods of nature and society, denouncing them as idols. Worship was to be reserved for the one true God above. But this disenchantment remained always partial. "There can be no society," Durkheim wrote, "which does not feel the need of upholding and reaffirming at regular intervals the collective sentiments and collective ideas which make its unity and its personality."[1] This upholding and affirming is not coldly rational. It draws upon the power of the sacred.

Durkheim's assessment of the relation of social authority to sacred authority is sociological, not theological, but it is not discordant with the biblical view. As Paul writes in his Letter to the Romans (13:1), "Let every person be subject to the governing authorities. For there is no authority except from God, and those that exist have been instituted by God." In Judeo-Christian tradition, governing powers are not deities, but their dictates are tinctured with divine legitimacy.

The same can be said for cultural norms. Wedding vows and public oaths invoke what is immutable and permanent to bind the changeable, fickle course of human events. Myth and legend accumulate to articulate the sacred sources of the social compact. Even modern countries such as the United States have Founding Fathers, mortal men with flaws, to be sure, but somehow imbued with an enduring authority. Monuments and memorials reach for the transcendent. Parades and civic celebrations are rituals, not religious in the sense in which we now use the term, but with a higher significance than everyday life.

The role of the sacred remained central in the West even as the authority of the Church was displaced. During the most advanced stages of the French Revolution, the Nabobs of the Empire of Reason instituted secular festivals and quasi-religious ceremonies to celebrate their new vision of humanity. New rituals replaced the old; secular deities of Rights and Reason superseded the God of the Bible. These Enlightenment gods were soon dethroned by new competitors such as empire and commerce. We can critique these modern gods—and we should; they are often false idols—but the sacralizing impulse in public life is fundamental. Our social consensus always reaches for transcendent legitimacy.

As Durkheim drew his theoretical analysis to a close, he reflected on the social conditions of Europe at the beginning of the twentieth century. The West was going through a transition. Thoughtful men no longer thrilled to "the great things of the past which filled our fathers with enthusiasm."[2] The old deities were losing their power. It was not just that the God of Christianity and Judaism, though influential in private devotions, was waning as the organizing authority for social life. The modern pantheon of Reason, Science, and Progress was losing its hold on the imaginations of men as well. These gods, once so powerful, had shown themselves to be impotent. Unjust inequalities endured. Men still suffered. And so the late nineteenth and early twentieth century was a time of ambivalence and uncertainty, a mood captured in the endlessly quoted line from W. B. Yeats: "Things fall apart; the center cannot hold." Loyalties were being withdrawn in the search for new but yet unfound devotions. "In a word," Durkheim wrote, "the old gods are growing old or already dead, and others are not yet born."[3]

One of the founders of modern social science, Durkheim was a man of great critical intelligence. He was tempted by a vision of knowing without believing. Yet it was precisely his critical powers and freedom from the pious illusions of rationalism that delivered him from the utopianism of imagining that societies can survive on facts without myths, on authority without rituals, and on reality without dreams. "This state of incertitude and confused agitation cannot last forever."[4] Men always rally around the sacred. There's nothing about modernity that changes this deep truth. "A day will come," he continued prophetically, "when our societies will know again those hours of creative effervescence."[5]

The old public theologies and civic rites will not be restored. "There are no gospels that are immortal," he observed.[6] This is not a theological statement, but rather a sociological one. Biblical religion can surely endure and its soulcraft will continue. It may even see a season of revival that enlarges its influence. I certainly hope it does. But it cannot resume its old place in society. The same is true for naïve Enlightenment pieties. "But neither is there any reason," Durkheim continued, "for believing humanity is incapable of inventing new ones."[7] The death of old gods in no way means the death of the sacred. We are social animals, and public life requires the aroma of the sacred. Durkheim admitted that he could not foresee what form the new gods would take, but he was right about the general trend. He died in 1917, living only long enough to see the first intimations of the gods who would storm through Europe with fire and steel.

The generation that lived through the years between 1914 and 1945 wished to put a stop to the socioreligious dynamic Durkheim identified. This was Popper's explicit project. He urged those who survived the war to forswear the impulse to seek sacred foundations for society, to be satisfied with meaning rather than truth. His cadres of leaders were to be "social technologists," not poets and orators. Hayek's approach differed. He prized the spontaneous order of the free market. It promised an order without authority, which is to say a society without gods. But his central judgment was the same as Popper's: the West can escape bloody cycles of self-destruction only if we stifle the all-too-human impulse to consolidate around shared loyalties.

The postwar consensus readily absorbed that view. It was widely believed that the cultural calamity of 1914–1945 required paradoxically strong medicine to weaken the power of the sacred to build loyalty and solidarity. This was an understandable response. Men do horrible things in the service of strong gods. Traditional societies justify radical inequalities, calling them expressions of sacred hierarchies. They demand terrible sacrifices for collective aims perfumed with transcendent claims. Modern societies have inflicted unspeakable brutalities in the service of utopian ideologies that claim the supreme sanction of History. Would it not be better to live without the strong gods, old or new? Isn't skeptical doubt safer than faith and devotion? Isn't a thoroughgoing and permanent critical disposition for the best? Aren't we better off with an anti-dogmatic spirit? If we must have gods, shouldn't they be weak, not strong: difference, dialogue, diversity, and other motifs of openness, or efficiency, productivity, and utility, the bloodless, technocratic metrics that leave us unmolested in our "little worlds"?

I sympathize with the postwar figures discussed in these pages. I, too, fear the power of the sacred in public life. Anyone who reads the Bible knows that divine power can annihilate as well as uplift, destroy as well as sanctify. But it is perilous to ignore certain truths about our humanity. Durkheim was right. To be human is to seek transcendent warrants and sacred sources for our social existence. As a consequence, a too rigorously anti-utopian outlook is itself dangerously utopian. Vattimo's conceit that the weakening of Being is the "destiny" of the West is dangerous in just this way, for the battle against ideological bewitchment and the authoritarian personality can become ruthlessly ideological in its own way: a totalitarianism of critique, a dictatorship of relativism. We see as much in the hectoring political correctness and the hardened and inflexible dogmas of the anti-dogmatic postwar consensus.

The strong gods are not golden idols or characters in ancient mythologies, as Durkheim recognized. They are whatever has the power to inspire love—love of the divine, love of truth, love of country, love of family. Love need not be social, at least not in its immediate object. The strong gods are not necessarily public or political. The desert monks of early Christianity sought union with God in the isolation of their cells. A mathematical genius can be a solitary slave to his love of the universal language of mathematics. But love is always eccentric. It impels us outside ourselves, breaking the boundaries of me-centered existence. Love seeks to unite with and rest in that which is loved. This outflowing of the self makes love the engine of solidarity. The strong gods of public life are quite simply the objects of our shared loves. They are whatever arouses in us an ardor to wed our destinies to that which we love.

We are made for love. We do not want to rest in our solitary selves or in our "little worlds." We desire to live shoulder to shoulder with our fellow man in the service of shared loves. So no, we are not safer with never-ending critique, the spontaneous order of the free market, technocratic management of utilities, and the other therapies of weakening. Disenchantment will not make our society more humane and hospitable. When the open society becomes an enemy of shared loves, when critical intelligence wages total war against our anchoring convictions, our spiritual, cultural, and political consensus becomes anti-human. This is what has happened in the West. The destiny of weakening works against the return of the strong gods, which means it works against love and solidarity. This loveless consensus is sparking populist revolts. It's why my young friend yearns for the end of the long twentieth century.

## Today's Anti-Politics

More than a few commentators treat our crisis as an illusion, a consequence of momentary derangements or foreign conspiracies. Duped by charlatans, British voters failed to see the obvious benefits of EU membership. But for Putin's machinations, Trump would not have won. But others see the crisis as real, the result of the economic changes that have broken the social contract established after World War II between labor and capital, or a response to unrestrained immigration. Some dig more deeply, identifying one or another spiritual malaise rooted in secularization and manifest in the low birthrates in Europe (and now in the United States as well), which bespeak a mentality that desires no future beyond the worldly self.

These explanations have greater or lesser merit, but it is important to recognize their anti-political logic. The diagnoses treat populism as an economic, psychological, moral, or even spiritual phenomenon. They shift attention away from political questions raised by populism, questions about national identity, immigration, and foreign policy, all of which cast doubt on the legitimacy of the established leadership class in the West. The strong gods preside over these questions, for they concern our common loves—loves which the powerful seem not to share. It is the animus against the strong gods and the poverty of love among our leadership class, an animus and poverty deliberately cultivated by the postwar open society consenus, that cause today's populism.

The pragmatic, end-of-ideology liberalism of the 1950s was an early manifestation of the shift away from political questions. Following Popper in spirit if not in detail, the shift was an attempt to drive out the strong gods that rally men to grand causes. The postwar era aimed at good economic and social management—governance by economic planners, psychological help from therapists, and cultural management by experts. These techniques were thought to be the best way to ensure increases in private utility, healthy adaptations to modern social conditions, and low-friction civic relations. The goal was a modest solidarity based on widely shared prosperity and general satisfaction with social conditions. This approach has been through many iterations in recent decades, but it is still with us. Today's technocratic ethos defines political legitimacy in terms of the weak gods of policy expertise, therapeutic delicacy when speaking of sensitive topics, and the rhetoric of diversity and other motifs of inclusion.

The anti-politics nurtured by the postwar consensus is also manifest in rote denunciations of populist challengers, who are invariably described as fascists or racists. Aristotle thought the essential form of political life is rational debate about which laws promote the happiness of the city's citizens. The imperatives of the open society short-circuit this debate by translating it into a conflict between pure good and pure evil. The translation is already evident in Popper, who frames the entire history of the West as a battle of the "open" against the "closed," a dichotomy that is now taken for granted. Commenting

on the rise of populism, the former British prime minister Tony Blair
has insisted, "Today, a distinction that often matters more than traditional right and left is open versus closed." He leaves no doubt on
which side virtue lies. "The open-minded see globalization as an
opportunity," while "the close-minded see the outside world as a
threat."[8] The issue of our time is not, therefore, political. It is moral-
therapeutic, even spiritual-apocalyptic. Populism does not question
the effects of globalization on the social contract. It is not challenging
the political judgment of ruling elites such as Blair. Instead, by his
way of thinking, populism frames a world-historical choice: open or
closed, liberal or fascist, reasonable or paranoid.

This Manichean mentality has grown stronger even as the catastrophe of 1914–1945 fades from living memory. The generation that
lived through World War II entertained nuanced accounts of the origins and nature of Nazism. *The Origins of Totalitarianism* by Hannah
Arendt is exemplary in this regard. Those who fought and suffered
during the harrowing years of Hitler's rule tolerated former Nazi party
members in public roles in Germany after the war. Curiously enough,
as time passed and the actual dangers receded, anti-fascism strengthened. As the postwar consensus increased its control over the political
and cultural imagination of the leadership class of the West, the fear
of resurgent fascism, racism, and other evils became more widespread
and the anti-totalitarian imperatives became more urgent. And so we
come to our own time. Most in the West are ideologically inert,
drugged by consumer abundance, atomized and deprived of traditional
institutions of solidarity. As one wit put it, people today are not marching in the streets seeking a final solution; they are in search of a final
sale. Yet, oddly, hysteria about the return of authoritarians and fascists
is widespread. This paranoia afflicts not ordinary people but elites, who
habitually characterize the political challenges posed by populism—
regarding the economy, immigration, and foreign policy—as

world-historical struggles of good against evil. This is as true in the United States as in Europe, though in America the danger is usually cast as a resurgence of racism and "hate."

The now conventional strategies of disenchantment support the anti-politics of the open society. People formed by the postwar consensus take concerns about the stability of the family in twenty-first-century America to be expressions of "patriarchy" or "heteronormativity." Patriotic appeals are "unmasked" as racist or xenophobic. We're often told that "Make America Great Again" *really* means "Make America White Again." In these and other ways, our leadership class treats unwelcome political challenges as phobias to be denounced rather than ideas to be grappled with on their own terms. These powerful mental habits are debilitating, making our leadership class less capable of leading, not only because they can't see reality but also because they transform political opposition to their rule into moral crimes.

In the undying twentieth century, the establishments of the West exacerbate our most pressing problems, all of which reflect a crisis of solidarity, rather than addressing them. Marriage is collapsing among working-class Americans. In the face of this reality, it borders on insanity to fix political attention on transgender bathrooms and other symbols of cultural deregulation. An epidemic of death by drug overdose is damaging communities and shattering families, and our leaders are pushing for marijuana legalization. As the suicide rate among unemployed men rises, we launch a crusade for doctor-assisted suicide. Poor neighborhoods are being denuded of functional civic organizations, religious or secular, and we sue the religious communities trying to serve them, seeking to compel conformity with the sexual revolution. All of this suggests our leadership class is so thoroughly blinded by the postwar consensus that the only problems it can see are those of discrimination, exclusion, and conformism—nails for their open-society hammer. Meanwhile, the actual problems we face—atomization, dissolving communal bonds, disintegrating family ties, and a nihilistic culture of limitless self-definition—go unaddressed. When someone does speak up about them, he is denounced.

The most important questions of our time therefore go unanswered. Can we make the global economy work for middling folks in the West? Are we able to restore a shared moral community that protects the undisciplined among us from self-destructive vices? How should we respond to mass migration? Should there be limits to globalization, and if so, set by whom and to what end? And then there is the fundamental question: What is the role of the nation in the twenty-first century?

These are not questions for the seminar room. They need to be at the center of public debate because they bear upon the future of the West. The cohort of foreign-born residents of the United States is now estimated at nearly 15 percent of the total population, the highest level in more than one hundred years. Under these circumstances, only a person ignorant of human nature, of man's innate desire for stability, familiarity, and continuity—a home—can cheerily reiterate the win-win promise of diversity. In some European countries, the strain is even greater because so many migrants are Muslim. There are always cultural and political limitations to pluralism, and a deconsolidated, fragmented nation can be as great a threat to human dignity as an over-consolidated, conformist one. In truth, it poses a far graver threat, as refugees from Syria can testify.

Some speak of the nation as a "recent invention." This is not an intellectually serious claim. The Old Testament tells us of the people of Israel. The notion of an English people claiming representation in a sovereign government goes back more than one thousand years. The history of nations in the West tells of struggles by the peoples of

Europe to attain suitable political forms. In 1648, the Peace of Westphalia brought an end to the European wars of religion by establishing formal norms of national sovereignty. The limited liability corporation was still some way off, but no one today dismisses it as a troublesome "recent invention," for it serves the ideals of openness, fluidity, and border-crossing that animate the metaphysical dreams of the postwar era. The nation, however, gets heavily critical treatment because, unlike the denizens of the marketplace, it evokes love and loyalty. This is just one example of the way in which the postwar consensus deprives us of the means to meet the challenges of the twenty-first century. At the end of his life, Samuel Huntington wrote a book about the American nation, *Who Are We? The Challenges to America's National Identity*. It was a prescient meditation on the issue we now face, yet it was denounced as xenophobic and crypto-racist when it was published.

In his memoir of public service during World War II and the Cold War, *Present at the Creation*, Dean Acheson reports that his mentor in the Roosevelt administration, Secretary of War Henry Stimson, insisted upon the importance of protectionist policies. Stimson was captive to the priorities of an earlier time when high tariffs allowed the United States to become an industrial power, an era that was brought to an end by a war that projected the Unites States into a new role in global affairs. Even before its entry into World War II, America had become the indispensable economic center for Allied resistance to fascism. After the war, as Acheson documents, leaders in Washington slowly came to realize that Soviet aggression meant American internationalism must continue, even grow. Old assumptions about trade, tariffs, and American involvement in international institutions had to be reexamined. The United States adopted a more globalist perspective as it organized and supported what came to be known as the "free world."

In 1950, as Acheson's memoir shows, free trade and other coalition-building policies became a priority, serving America's national interest in the years that followed, just as isolationism and protectionism had done in the early twentieth century, when Stimson's convictions were formed. As Acheson knew, circumstances had changed, and the priorities of U.S. foreign policy had to change as well. What remained constant, however, was the guiding principle of promoting America's national interest, which after 1945 was implicated in a complex international struggle against communist imperialism.

We are living through another period of changing circumstances—not as dramatic as World War II and the Cold War, but significant nonetheless. As I argued in the last chapter, economic globalization has broken the alignment between the economic and political interests of social classes in the West. During World War II, American elites depended for their very survival on factory workers to build ships, planes, and tanks, just as the workers depended on the leadership class to bring victory rather than defeat and slavery. This reciprocal dependency was a powerful source of the solidarity that persisted in the years after World War II, which is why those who came of age in the 1950s remember it as a time of unity and common purpose. Global trade and the free flow of capital slowly eroded this solidarity, especially the bond between the leaders and those they led. After 1989 the erosion accelerated. Today, Apple does not need high school–educated Americans. It outsources. It does not even need Ph.D.s. They are happy to import them with H-1B visas.

Apple is a company, not a civic organization. It is not responsible for civic health, at least not directly. But corporate behavior is one sign among many that the "rules-based international order" and the global economic system it sustains no longer serve America's national interest, at least not in obvious ways. A democratic society requires economic solidarity. In the modern era this means nurturing a recip-rocal dependency that knits together the fates of labor and capital, the interests of ordinary workers and the "creative class." As economic solidarity declines, leaders often respond to incentives that distract them from serving the interests of those whom they lead. The punch-ing-down rhetoric of recent years—"takers," "deplorables," "fly-over country"—strongly suggests that this has happened. Yet the prestige of openness and weakening is so great that our establishment cannot recognize this as a problem, much less address it effectively. Popper's thought and the imperatives of the open society leave no room for the concept of the nation and the cultural solidarity it nurtures. Hayek and the free-market imperatives can't make any sense of the notion of economic solidarity either. Milton Friedman suggests that wanting to encourage such a thing is "collectivism," tantamount to slavery.

The cultural and political challenges facing the West in the twenty-first century require our leadership class to ask questions they have been trained to suppress. We are threatened not by militant nationalism but by profound global pressures—not only economic pressures, but also those of mass migration. Cultural deregulation and the rhetoric of weakening make ordinary people wonder whether their leaders care for the nations of which they are citizens. This altogether reasonable anxiety is reinforced by the globalist utopia-nism mouthed by so many: open trade, open borders, and open minds. When the establishment talks this way, it stokes disquietude.

Our leaders feel unmanned by today's challenges because our problems are the consequences of the ascendant postwar consensus. It has deconsolidated and opened up economic and cultural life to a remarkable degree. Much has been achieved since 1945 that we should want to preserve. We don't want to go back to militarism, totalitarian regimes, and vicious racial segregation. But in the main, the successes of the postwar era have sidelined questions of solidarity, as Popper and Hayek wished. Not surprisingly, that which has been neglected has decayed, producing the problems of our time, all of which touch upon the essential question of public life, the one Huntington recognized as requiring attention: Who are we? What are the loves we share? What communal loyalties properly demand sacrifice? Who among us belongs to the "we"?

Popper and Hayek and the subsequent postwar consensus rule out these questions, for they call for the return of the strong gods. They are questions that must not be asked in an open society, much less answered, for they lead, we are warned, to fascism and racism. For the free-market libertarian, the miracle of spontaneous order excuses us from asking or answering the question of the "we." Free trade will knit the world together. Something like the Paul Samuelson theory of price-factor equalization shows that the market will eventually sort out the disequilibria brought about by globalization. If we are just patient, the market will solve our political problems, which means we don't really need politics at all.

### The Indispensable Pronoun

Popper and Hayek understood that Durkheim was correct about the role of the gods. In every political culture, the "we" touches upon sacred things. Human beings are by nature social animals. But the particularity of the "we" is always a gift. Patrimony comes unbidden. I was created in the image and likeness of God, a noble heritage I share with every other human being. But in that universal inheritance I did not receive my distinctive patrimony as a "Reno." That came by accident. If I were from another family, I would still enjoy all the dignity of the humanity I share with others, but I would not be a "Reno." And yet I do not feel the contingency as a diminishment. My parents, grandparents, and ancestors before them are in a real sense far more necessary to me than my generic humanity, so much so that I'm far more likely to sacrifice my life for my blood relations than for someone outside the family circle, however equal he may be in the eyes of God. This is at once an obvious point about human nature—blood is thicker than water, as folk wisdom puts it—and something remarkable. The miracle of the "we" turns contingent familial solidarity into something more precious than our universal humanity. It is so powerful that it can overcome genetic differences, which is to say nature herself. Marriage creates a "we." Adoption can expand the "we." There is something thicker than blood—the union of shared loves.

The miracle of the "we" infuses political solidarity with sacred significance. We are not created American or English or Polish, but our native languages are beloved. It's not simply a metaphor to speak of our motherlands and fatherlands. Here as well the power of the "we" transcends biology. Nations unite clans and tribes, villages and provinces. They can incorporate newcomers by "naturalizing" them, a process of civic adoption, as it were. And, of course, religious communities manifest the sacred sources of "we" as well, for they come from a divine source.

The solidarity found in the "we" is always political in the broadest sense. Because the "we" is not natural—that is, it is not simply a consequence of our shared humanity or a biological dynamic of genetic connection—its particularity requires intentional effort to create, guide, and sustain. In short, the "we" does not just happen. I must form a domestic bond with a woman and have a child to perpetuate my family name. The civic realm needs to be defended; its history must be passed down, and the native language has to be taught. All this and much more must be done if a "we" is to have a future. Revelation and tradition have to be passed down and children catechized to sustain the religious "we."

In every such endeavor, individuals must exercise their freedom. The "we" is not the product of a calculation of utility, nor is it simply given in racial or any other genetically determined identity. The "we" is an end in itself that asks us to do what is necessary to sustain and promote our shared loves, all of which harken to the call of strong gods. Governance, therefore, is integral to the "we." In the intimate affairs of domestic life, it is obvious that the decisions and initiatives of the husband and wife allow the family to flourish. Let us leave aside religious leadership, which is explicitly ordered to the service of the divine, and focus on political leadership and the sacred sources of the civic "we."

In its classical definition, a republic is not merely a system of government. It is that which is held as a common good among a particular people, a *res publica*. The *res*—the common thing that is the object of a shared love—is often many-sided. The French cherish their language and assign to their public institutions responsibility for maintaining its integrity and purity. The English are loyal to their free institutions, their history, and their countryside. Postwar Germans are disquieted by their own uncertainty about whether they have a right to be proud of their history. One could go on and on describing national characters. Better, however, to adopt a more general definition of the "shared thing." In his massive account of world history, *The City of God*, Augustine defines the "we" as "an assembled multitude of rational creatures bound together by a common agreement as to the objects of their love."

The postwar consensus is, at root, fearful of love. Formed by the decades of catastrophe, the generation so ably represented by Popper and Hayek recognized that love's passions can lead to destructive devotions. Love enflames ambitions, some of which impel us toward evil ends. Love inspires sacrifices, some of which are misguided and self-destructive. At their worst, perverse loves can beckon us to sacrifice others.

Our consensus in favor of openness seeks to prevent these dangers by depriving us of love's objects. Its techniques of disenchantment and weakening try to banish the strong gods or at least make them too weak to rouse our hearts. The postwar consensus critiques, deconstructs, and deflates a great deal of what the Western tradition has championed as fitting objects of our love—not only God, but the nation and our cultural inheritance, even truth itself. By certain measures, the postwar consensus has been remarkably successful. It has brought calm to the West and great wealth as well. Since 1945 there has been but one war in Europe—on the margins, in the Balkans—the consequence of passions and collective grievances stirred up by the collapse of the artificially imposed unity of communism. Its destructive, tribal passions seemed to vindicate the love-weary skepticism of Popper, Hayek, and the rest.

An open-society calm continues to dampen dangerous upsurges of discontent in the core nations of the West. Protesters regularly march through Paris. Italy can seem ungovernable. Germany anguishes over its history. Populism roils elections. Yet no paramilitary organizations—no Black Shirts, Brown Shirts, or Red Brigades—are taking to the streets. Anti-globalization riots in Hamburg in 2017 were softened by an atmosphere of protest tourism rather than earnest rebellion. Local residents fed protestors sandwiches. Governing authorities seemed vaguely sympathetic. After all, in the atmosphere of the postwar consensus, street protests are presumptively beneficial. They remind us of the virtues of the open society, which are worth the broken windows and burning cars. After Trump's election, the people who took to the streets were overwrought women in ridiculous hats. Vattimo is right: There has been a great weakening. These days the occasional episodes of street violence are often the work of anti-fascist gangs who relish the rare opportunities our age allows for strong actions insofar as they target whatever remains of the historical enemies of the open society—political correctness with cudgels.

But the project of peace without love cannot go on much longer. Man was not created to be alone. We do not desire calm, not even when satiated by countless pleasures. We yearn to join ourselves to others, not only in the bond of matrimony but in civic and religious bonds as well. The "we" arises out of love, a ferocious power that seeks to rest in something greater than oneself. In the first half of the twentieth century, perverse loves destroyed a great deal in the West, not just lives and buildings, but cultural legitimacy as well. It is not surprising that Popper's open society and Hayek's spontaneous market order gained the upper hand. Nevertheless, the death camps, gulags, atomic bombs, and killing fields, however horrible, did not destroy human nature. Our hearts remain restless. They seek to rest in loyalty to strong gods worthy of love's devotion and sacrifice. And our hearts will find what they seek.

### The Way Forward

The concerns that drive populism in the West—immigration, borders, and national sovereignty—reflect a growing sense that the "we" needs shoring up, which means calling upon the strong gods to renew our shared loves. Populism is antiestablishment because our leadership class refuses to renew the "we." Instead of guiding and refining the populist calls for love and loyalty, it bears down on them with disenchantment and weakening.

This response is not entirely wrong. Perverse loves of dark gods that rise from below present real dangers. Unfortunately, these debasing loves are easily fueled by the chthonian preoccupation with race and sex that dominates in so many progressive circles. White nationalism makes sense in an open-society consensus that has reduced so much to biology. But these perverse loves do not create a "we." They do not require free activity to sustain and promote a shared love. They are gods of identity, not of political community. The descendants of slaves in the United States constitute a "we" that shares a historical memory and seeks a common flourishing. That memory and that flourishing require human agency, for what has been endured must be retold, and the bonds of solidarity must be renewed. By contrast, the brute fact of shared skin color requires no such human agency, although in the artificial environment of universities an ersatz "we" has formed around grievances and theories of systemic injustice. The same is true for the gay "community." To some degree, a "we" exists in the pursuit of legal equality and social acceptance. But once achieved, the solidarity of shared sexual practices is not a political project. In truth, the anti-political trajectory is a sure sign of debasing loves. It was not a coincidence that Nazism had no use for the state and its mechanisms of governance, seeking instead to rule through the Party and the Leader. The movement aspired to be a direct expression of German identity unmediated by politics.

The perverse gods of blood, soil, and identity cannot be overcome with the open-society therapies of weakening. On the contrary, they are *encouraged* by multiculturalism and the reductive techniques of critique. In its present decadent form, the postwar consensus makes white nationalism an entirely cogent position. Based in the "little world" of DNA, it asserts its claim to recognition in the acclaimed celebration of diversity. We cannot forestall the return of the debasing gods by reapplying the open-society imperatives. False loves can be remedied only by true ones. A humane future in the West will require nurturing noble loves.

We have resources in our tradition that will help us to do so. Drawing on classical sources, Augustine observed that the ancient Romans were united in a two-fold love—the love of freedom and the love of honor. The freedom Romans loved was not individual freedom but the freedom of the city, the liberty of a people to make its own laws and embark on its own projects. The Roman Republic was free insofar as it ran its own affairs and resisted the dominion of foreign powers. This love of self-government remains strong for most peoples of the West. It sparked the nationalist revolutions that spelled the end of empires in the modern era. It is the basis for skepticism about the European Union and other supranational institutions.

If it is "nationalist" to cherish self-government, then we should be nationalists. The strong god of self-government and sovereignty, which calls upon us to use our freedom and reason, is ennobling. Aristotle sometimes says that politics is the highest good. He makes this judgment because we are rational animals, which is why in other places he says that contemplation is the highest good. But most of us are not cut out for contemplation, and even if we are, we've got day jobs. Politics has the advantage of being of immediate concern. Because the laws of the land affect me and my interests, I am moved to deliberate with my fellow lawmakers. My participation in political debate then draws me toward consideration of the common good and how to formulate the best and most fitting laws for the body politic, not just for me.

In Aristotle's time, only the well-born few voted on laws. In modern democracies, by contrast, all citizens are implicated in the political process. This universal participation has not been an unequivocal good—mass politics is a breeding ground for ideologies offering cookie-cutter formulas that appear to avoid the uncertainties of fallible political reason—but on the whole, a politicized populace is a blessing. By drawing the many into the affairs of state, however remotely, democracy encourages them to transcend their me-centered existence. The strong god of the nation draws us out of our "little worlds." Our shared loves—love of our land, our history, our founding myths, our warriors and heroes—raise us to a higher vantage point. We see our private interest as part of a larger whole, the "we" that calls upon our freedom to serve the body politic with intelligence and loyalty. As Aristotle recognized, this loyalty is intrinsically fulfilling, for it satisfies the human desire for transcendence.

Anyone who denies that a nation of more than 300 million people can practice democratic self-governance in any meaningful sense underestimates the power of the "we." When seventy thousand football fans rise for the national anthem, their reverence is repaid with pride—pride in *their* country. I find myself increasingly impatient with those who despise patriotic ceremonies and traditions. Invariably educated and well-off, they have personal assets and achievements to be proud of. But most Americans are not so self-satisfied. Their proudest achievement is the freedom of their country; their most precious possession is their citizenship; their most important contribution to self-government is their loyalty. Patriotism renews the bond of the "we." True, only a few actually make the laws in our nation. But insofar as this vast nation is united as a "we," politics in America, however messy, is about governing a people rather than the technocratic management of various interests.

Modern liberal theorists have worked hard to show that self-interest can be the basis of shared loves in a republic. Thomas Hobbes, for example, noting that everyone has an interest in not dying, argued that the perils of a violent world would move men to give their unqualified loyalty to the sovereign who promises to protect them. John Locke, whose view of the state of nature was less gloomy than Hobbes's, argued that each man's interest in his personal freedom and private property is reasonable grounds for his consent to the authority of a government that will defend those interests.

These and other liberal theories shape our political imaginations. They are called "liberal" because they seek to identify a basis for civic loyalty in self-interest. I enter into the "we" by my free decision to secure my person (Hobbes) and to secure my freedom of thought and action and my property (Locke). These liberal theories suggest a useful test of the strong gods of public life: Are they humanizing or dehumanizing? Do they lay waste or bring flourishing? Shared loves that abandon individuals to the rapacious, dominating, bloodthirsty impulses of others are surely malevolent, as are the strong gods that imprison on whim, employ thought police, and confiscate property.

These liberal theories are me-centered only in part. The liberal democratic ethos does not want freedom only in the Roman sense of collective freedom from domination and for self-government. It also values a public spirit of voluntariness: This is my country not merely because I was born here, for if I could, I would actively choose it. The common good of widespread consent to our way of life affects civic affairs in many ways. It is obviously manifest in an all-volunteer military. But in more subtle ways the atmosphere of consent—*I'm here because I want to be here!*—fuses private interests with public spiritedness. It allows our commercial republic to be both an arena for the pursuit of wealth and self-interest and a genuine republic, a commonwealth we care about for its own sake and which we are willing to sustain, defend, and improve, even at the cost of personal sacrifice.

The United States is a place to which countless people have actively *chosen* to come. Immigration plays a central role in our history. But consent does not supersede love, and we should never let ourselves be bewitched by liberal theories into thinking that reasoned defenses for a system of government give life to a people. The ceremony by which immigrants become citizens is called naturalization. It ascribes paternity. We do not consent to our parents. Our paternity is not the consequence of reasoned assent. The same holds for our political and cultural inheritance, whether bestowed at birth or acquired later in what is best understood as civic adoption. The "we" is never confected out of shared choices. It is always a gift conferred by shared loves. The objects of our loves in a real sense choose us, not we them.

As I have emphasized, a true "we" calls for my loyalty, my active vigilance in sustaining a shared way of life. It is imperative that we recover this active vigilance, which has been overlooked, even discouraged, by the postwar consensus. We need to return again and again to the fundamental questions of public life: Who are we? What kind of people have we been and do we wish to become? These questions require ongoing conversation, not short creedal statements, and certainly not a DNA test. In an era of mass immigration and demographic change, it is more important than ever to have this conversation in the West. It needs to include more than our modern democratic traditions. The question of who we are must take biblical religion into account. It has to do justice to the land and its influence on our collective imagination. The "we" has many historical strands and local instantiations. The "we" in Mobile, Alabama, is not the same at the "we" in Seattle, Washington—though both are American. This is not a conversation that can be conducted under the police surveillance of political correctness. We need to learn to speak again of the loves we share, not the injustices we reject or the exclusions we renounce.

Populism reflects the instinct in the citizens of the West to escape the death grip of the postwar consensus and the contradictions of the open society, which commands us to "celebrate diversity" and "promote inclusion." These can be fitting imperatives under some circumstances, but as shibboleths they impede political discussion of who we are. Identity politics is another cancer. It assumes that we cannot transcend our tribe, so we need the postmodern experts and diversity consultants to manage our differences. At the same time, libertarian economists reduce the body politic to an economic machine. In a more upbeat mood, multiculturalism promises a "play of difference" that will bring ever-greater innovation, creativity, and human fulfillment. But whether pinched or utopian, the postwar consensus deters us from talking about what really matters in the twenty-first century—our shared loves.

Popper saw the open society as a metaphysical-spiritual project, not just a political one. It requires the weakening of truth and demands from us an asceticism that renounces the warmth of shared loves—a willingness to endure the "strain" of knowing that we give history meaning. This project cannot be opposed solely on political grounds, as if nationalism alone can overcome the "destiny of weakening." We need strengthening motifs across the board. A man who cannot affirm the border between male and female will find it difficult to defend a border between nations. Those who shrink from the strong god of truth are sure to see danger rather than blessing in the strong god of patriotism.

The twentieth century will end only when we entertain new metaphysical dreams, dreams of strengthening rather than weakening. For too long we have favored a critical sensibility that is reductive. It consistently goes "down." For example, young people assigned Virgil's *Aeneid* are encouraged to talk about imperialism. Or discussions of America's founding fixate on slavery or other injustices. In general, we engage in seemingly endless preparatory conversations about "privilege" or worry about the structures of oppression that infect our very words. (For decades we've anxiously debated pronouns rather than reflecting on what it means to be a man or a woman.)

The more scientifically minded are only too likely to reduce classical questions of truth, beauty, and justice to the play of economic interests or to speculate about the blind cleverness of selfish genes. This mode of analysis gains approbation as "objective."

But this is not the critical sensibility of Plato's dialogues or the Old Testament prophets. In its classical mode, critical thinking goes "up." It disenchants the half-truths of conventional wisdom so that a fuller truth can shine forth. It exposes contradictions and smashes idols so that we can look upward with fresh eyes. It seeks a strengthening of Being, not its weakening. If we are to meet the challenges of the twenty-first century, we must recover this kind of critical reason. Our conversations about what it means to be a man or a woman must illuminate human nature. We must entertain metaphysical arguments about the nature and existence of God. The strong gods will make their return only in an atmosphere of strengthening. We need truth, not meaning, if we are to test and purify their claims to our love.

When it comes to the strong gods of public life, we are sure to go wrong. Modernity encourages us to give our hearts to politics and the nation, which is why ideological passions are so easily triggered. We easily imagine the nation as more than our civic home; it is our savior. To combat this idolatry, we need to nurture two primeval sources of solidarity that limit the claims of the civic "we": the domestic society of marriage and the supernatural community of the church, synagogue, and other communities of transcendence.

Today, marriages are often broken by divorce or temporary partnership. Nevertheless, people find ways to be together for holidays. They fall back on family in times of difficulty. It is always so. The family shelters; the family gives rest. As we shepherd the return of the strong gods, it is essential that we do what we can to restore domestic stability. There is a political component to this restoration. Tax and employment policies can have an effect on the margins. It might be worth revisiting no-fault divorce. But cultural politics are more important. The first principle must be to do no harm. Men and women are naturally drawn together by erotic desire and an instinct for domesticity. We need to combat the radical feminism that is hostile to even the weakest expressions of distinct male and female roles in courtship and marriage. Just as we need a national conversation about who we are, we need a sober conversation about what it means to be a man and a woman.

I am a Catholic. I'd like to see a widespread revival of Christianity in the West. Until that happens, unbelievers need to wake up to the perils of a faithless society. Before 1945, most liberal writers and leaders recognized that a healthy political culture depends on the vitality of communities of faith that transcend politics. They identified the moral discipline inculcated by religious communities as a key ingredient of a healthy society. That's important, but more important still is the rest that religious faith provides in the modern era.

Belief in transcendence provides powerful consolations in the face of injustice, suffering, and death. In religious faith, one is at home in the most fundamental sense, resting in God's arms, protected from the slings and arrows of temporal life. This security can make religious believers stable and stalwart citizens, less likely to be inflamed by ideological promises that are surrogates for true religion. Religious believers are also able to endure the trials that every nation and people must suffer on the slaughter bench of history. It sounds contradictory, but a strongly transcendent faith grounds a person.

Public life, domestic life, and religious life: these are what Russell Hittinger has called the three "necessary societies." The strong gods are returning in the public realm, animating the populism that seeks to restore the nation. If we are to encourage this restoration of solidarity with intelligence, we must pursue a wider strategy of strengthening. Throughout the history of the West, communities of transcendence have pinioned the nation from above, while the marital and domestic bonds of family loyalty have pinioned it from below. Let us learn from this history: The best safeguards against the dangers of love's perversion are the loves that ennoble and give us rest. The solidarities of domestic life and religious community are not at odds with the civic "we." On the contrary, the strong gods can reinforce each other, preparing our hearts for love's many devotions. A man who makes sacrifices for his family or for his faith is likely to be ready to give the full measure of devotion to his country.

We need a spirit of devotion in our unsteady times. And it can be found more readily than we imagine. When I was a college student studying one summer in Germany, I read *Notes of a Native Son* by James Baldwin, a black American who tried to expatriate himself to France to escape America's racism. The book's introduction relates Baldwin's anguished recognition that he could not be anything other than the son of a country that would neither love him nor release him. Young and still overly impressed with the very American ideology of individualism, I was blindsided by the power of the "we." Alone in a strange land, I saw that I was Baldwin's brother. I too am a native son.

I felt the power of the "we" with even greater force more than two decades later. My church in Omaha was formed by the merger of an all-black parish and an all-white parish. One of the church leaders, a recently retired black man, arranged a screening of a film about the "Tuskegee Airmen," the all-black flight squadron in World War II. Required to serve in a racially segregated unit, they trained at a military base in the Deep South, where they were subjected to the humiliations of Jim Crow. When the film ended, the church leader stood to start a discussion. He was crying. The small group was not sure how to react. Then he asked, in an agonizing voice, "How could we have treated those men that way?"

It was an extraordinary moment, a revelation of the power of the "we." Before me stood a black man who was old enough to have grown up under segregation. And yet he felt that he was implicated in the racial injustices of white Americans. His tears were the fearsome gift of the strong gods. Out of many, they make us one. They use love's up-reaching power to bind us together, black and white, richer and poorer, in sickness and in health.

I am increasingly convinced that our political upheavals reflect a crisis of the postwar consensus, which socializes us to regard our highest duty as preventing the return of the strong gods and the gifts of solidarity they bring. To insist upon the weakening and disenchantment that banished the strong gods from the postwar West is profoundly wrongheaded and will bring woe, not peace. For deprived of true and ennobling loves, of which the patriotic ardor is surely one, people will turn to demagogues and charlatans who offer them false and debasing loves.

Our task, therefore, is to restore public life in the West by developing a language of love and a vision of the "we" that befits our dignity and appeals to our reason as well as to our hearts. We must attend to the strong gods who come from above and animate the best of our traditions. Only that kind of leadership will forestall the return of the dark gods who rise up from below.

# Afterword

J ust a few years after Germany's defeat in the Second World War, Ernst Jünger reflected on the disasters of the first half of the twentieth century. In a pensive essay, "Crossing the Line," he observed that a conservative attitude "can no longer arrest or divert the growing movement, as still seemed possible after the First War." A great deal had been swept away, not just by the war, but also by powerful economic forces that were mobilizing societies for the ends of production as never before. Conservatism, he continued, "always has to find itself a base in parts of the terrain that have not yet begun to move, such as the monarchy, the nobility, the army, the land. But once everything begins to slip there is no longer a point of support." Jünger felt that the West was becoming endlessly mobile, liquid, and insubstantial. "Unser Bestand"—a formulation that means our inventory or inheritance, the basis on which we can continue—"is moving as a whole across the critical line."[1] What once seemed to be solid ground on which to stand has crossed over into total mobilization, impermanence, and flux. We have no *Bestand*—no home—no basis on which and from which to reconstitute our dissolved world.

Jünger allowed that the unsheltered individual can, perhaps, find that "point of support" deep within himself as he walks remote "forest paths." But his assessment of the social conditions in the postwar West remained grim. His pessimism was understandable. He had miraculously survived four years of combat on the Western Front during World War I, lived through the political and moral collapse of Germany, and witnessed its physical ruin. His warning was fitting. The modern era has been one of disenchantment, as Max Weber and so many others recognized. Perhaps this has been the case since St. Peter preached after Pentecost. There is more than a sliver of truth in the radical theologies of the postwar era that saw in Christianity the demolition of the old, stable cosmos with God at the top of the great chain of being and everything in its appointed place below. Jünger saw our predicament with clarity. Today, it can seem that our inheritance is available only as a consumer product marketed by Ralph Lauren or that it exists only in nostalgic dreams, vivid in our imaginations but not available in the social reality in which we live.

Jünger warned against "defeatism," but his pessimism was too one-sided, like so many of the responses to the catastrophes of 1914–1945. Presuming that the traumas of the first half of the twentieth century fundamentally altered the conditions of human existence, we have adopted a destructive radicalism. Sometimes that radicalism is redemptive, as are diversity-talk, multiculturalism, and libertarian dreams of anarchic order brought about by the market mechanism. At other times that radicalism is surgical, an attempt to cut away the cancerous tumor that is killing the West— liberalism or nominalism, perhaps, or some other wrong turn. The postwar consensus and its meta-history of discontinuity—open versus closed—encourage this radicalism. Postwar conservatism, influenced by the unhealthy, apocalyptic, all-or-nothing atmosphere, is tempted by a parallel radicalism, which concludes that all is lost. Everything has crossed over into dissolution.

But that is not true. Let us renounce the twentieth century's false hold on our imaginations. The decades of catastrophe between 1914 and 1945 were not able to destroy everything worth sustaining. Monstrous men perpetrated great evils. Many were killed. But they failed to destroy the living practice of Torah. The synagogue endures. What began with Abraham continues. And because God's chosen people did not cross the line, the last century failed to sever the nerve of Western culture. Let us reckon with this profound truth and apply it to our own time. The one-sided extremism of the open-society consensus—punitive political correctness, undiluted liberalism, and unfettered free markets—has done great damage. But it has not destroyed everything we love.

The twentieth-century conceit that the fabric of the West had been torn in two is false. *Unser Bestand* is always damaged, always wasted and betrayed. It is always moving across the line. Ever since Adam fell, the noble, the true, and the worthy have been slipping toward dissolution. And yet our inheritance remains always available. Even in a decayed, demoralized society, a woman can have a child. Parental love may be damaged by a ruined culture of marriage, but it blossoms nonetheless. A young man finds himself under fire in a distant land and he discovers that he is more loyal to his comrades than to his own survival. The *Shema* is recited after Auschwitz, which reminds us that even ruined churches can be renewed. We may lack the words and have forgotten the names, but disenchantment is never complete. The line is never fully crossed. The sacred always calls to us. The strong gods return, renewing our inheritance, giving us a place to stand. So, as the last century ends, we need to face the future with a proper sense of what has been lost, yes, but also with confidence that something remains to nurture, love, and pass down to our children. Let us not be faint of heart in the twenty-first century, which is finally beginning.

And let us not be paralyzed by pessimism. In the early 1990s, when the West was flush with confidence after its triumph over communism, Aleksandr Solzhenitsyn warned against a superficial view of progress that lifts from our shoulders the burdens of political responsibility. "It is up to us," he wrote, "to stop seeing Progress (which cannot be stopped by anyone or anything) as a stream of unlimited blessings, and to view it rather as a gift from on high, sent down for an extremely intricate trial of our free will."[2] The same holds for a superficial view of inevitable regress, which can tempt conservatives as strongly as the idol of progress tempts progressives.

The postwar era is over. The time of openness and weakening is ending. Much has been lost—first in an orgy of violence and then in a compensatory assault on love, an assault that has gone much too far. This loss has been sent down from on high as an extremely intricate trial of our free will. Repairing *unser Bestand*, our home and inheritance, will be painfully difficult. Our task is to use our freedom and intelligence in doing so. We must return to the terrain that can be stabilized, though never finally fixed. This is a religious, cultural, and political task. It is ours.

# Acknowledgements

I would like to thank Robert Burch, Timothy Fuller, Conor Grubaugh, Mark Henrie, Edward Nowak, and Matt Rose, readers of early drafts and sources of encouragement. They assured me that I'm probably not wrong and might even be right about the past seventy-five years. They warned me that I come up short in the final chapter. True, indeed. As a child of what came before, my own voice has been weakened and my eyes dimmed.

I'm also indebted to Tom Spence. He convinced me that my essay "Return of the Strong Gods," published in *First Things*, merited fuller development. Following Tom's advice, I learned a great deal about the historical roots of today's neo-liberal fusion of cultural deregulation and free-market expansion. Rereading Karl Popper and Friedrich Hayek in the twenty-first century was especially rewarding. It is for the reader to decide whether Tom was wise to encourage me to dilate at book length on the strong gods and their return.

This essay in intellectual journalism lacks scholarly rigor in the attribution of sources. But I must flag two recent books that directly influenced my thinking about postwar America: Yuval Levin's *The Fractured Republic: Renewing America's Social Contract in the Age of*

167

*Individualism* and James Piereson's *Shattered Consensus: The Rise and Decline of America's Postwar Political Order*.

Finally, I'd like to offer a special thanks to my colleague John Varacalli. He guided me toward Durkheim's concluding reflections in *The Elementary Forms of Religious Life*. It was while reading Durkheim that I realized how deeply indebted to Philip Rieff is this undertaking in cultural-historical analysis. I have learned from him a great deal, not the least of which is the peril of despair.

# Notes

## Introduction

1. Richard Weaver, Letter to John and Esther Randolph, August 25, 1945. For a useful account of Weaver's response to fascism and the methods of "total war," see Robert H. Brinkmeyer Jr., "Richard Weaver, Lillian Smith, The Sought, and the World," *Oxford Handbook of the Literature of the U.S. South* (New York: Oxford University Press, 2016).
2. Richard Weaver, *Ideas Have Consequences* (Chicago: University of Chicago Press, 1948), 18.
3. Philip Stephens, "Boris Johnson and the Flight to English Nationalism," *Financial Times*, October 4, 2018.

## Chapter One

1. Karl Popper, *The Open Society and Its Enemies* (London: George Routledge & Sons, 1945), 2 vols.
2. Popper, *The Open Society and Its Enemies*, vol. 1, 1.
3. Ibid., vol. 1, 91.
4. Ibid., vol. 1, 96.
5. Ibid.
6. Ibid., vol. 1, 150.
7. Ibid., vol. 1, 152.
8. Ibid., vol. 2, 8.
9. Ibid., vol. 2, 24.
10. Ibid., vol. 1, 30.
11. Ibid., vol. 2, 210.

12. Ibid., vol. 2, 265.

13. Ibid.

14. Ibid.

15. Hillary D. Rodham's 1969 Student Commencement Speech, Wellesley College, https://www.wellesley.edu/events/commencement/archives/1969commencement/studentspeech.

16. Walter Lippmann, *Essays in the Public Philosophy* (Boston: Little, Brown, 1955).

17. These quotations are taken from George Marsden's helpful discussion of Lippmann and his critics, *The Twilight of the American Enlightenment* (New York: Basic Books, 2014), 43–56.

18. T. W. Adorno, Else Frenkel-Brunswik, Daniel J. Levinson, and R. Nevitt Sanford, *The Authoritarian Personality* (New York: Harper & Brothers, 1950).

19. Adorno et al., *The Authoritarian Personality.*, 1.

20. Ibid., 971.

21. Ibid.

22. Ibid., 975.

23. Ibid., 976.

24. Ibid., 975.

25. F. A. Hayek, *The Road to Serfdom* (Chicago: University of Chicago Press, 1944).

26. Hayek, *The Road to Serfdom*, 2.

27. Ibid., 17.

28. Ibid., 59.

29. Ibid., 57.

30. Ibid., 141–42.

31. Ibid., 36.

32. William F. Buckley Jr., *God and Man at Yale* (Washington: Regnery, 2002). Fiftieth Anniversary Edition.

33. Buckley Jr., *God and Man at Yale*, 142.

34. Ibid., 144–45.

35. Ibid., 158.

36. Austin W. Bramwell surveys the hostile reviews in his introduction to the Fiftieth Anniversary Edition, pp. xi–xix, as does Buckley in his introduction to the Twenty-Fifth Anniversary Edition (Washington: Regnery, 1977), xxi–lxii.

37. Buckley Jr., *God and Man at Yale* (Washington: Regnery, 1977), xliii.

# Chapter Two

1. Committee on the Objectives of a General Education in a Free Society, *General Education in a Free Society: The report of the Harvard Committee* (Cambridge, Mass.: Harvard University Press, 1945). The passage quoted is from the introduction by James Bryant Conant, x.
2. Committee on the Objectives of a General Education in a Free Society, *General Education in a Free Society.*, 50.
3. Ibid., 44.
4. Ibid., 51.
5. Sigmund Freud, *Civilization and Its Discontents*, trans. James Strachey (New York: W. W. Norton, 1961).
6. Freud, *Civilization and Its Discontents*, 101.
7. Ibid., 33.
8. The passages quoted are from Hutchins's preface to *The Great Conversation*, the first volume of the series *Great Books of the Western World* (Chicago: Encyclopaedia Britannica, 1952).
9. Hayek, *Road to Serfdom*, 218.
10. Albert Camus, *The Plague*, trans. Stuart Gilbert (New York: Knopf, 1948). Citations are to the paperback edition (New York: Vintage, 1991).
11. Camus, *The Plague*, 228.
12. Ibid., 253.
13. Ibid., 179.
14. Ibid., 132.
15. Ibid., 133.
16. Milton Friedman, *Capitalism and Freedom* (Chicago: University of Chicago Press, 1962). Citations are to the Fortieth Anniversary Edition (Chicago: University of Chicago Press, 2002).
17. Friedman, *Capitalism and Freedom*, 1.
18. Ibid., 1–2.
19. Ibid., 13.
20. Ibid., 23.
21. Ibid.
22. Ibid., 24.
23. Ibid.
24. Ibid.
25. Jacques Derrida, "Structure, Sign and Play in the Discourse of the Human Sciences," in *Writing and Difference*, trans. Alan Bass (Chicago: University of Chicago Press, 1978), 279.
26. Derrida, "Structure, Sign and Play in the Discourse of the Human Sciences, 292.
27. Ibid., 292.

28. Ibid.

29. Benoît Peeters, *Derrida: A Biography* (Cambridge, Mass.: Polity Press, 2013), 301.

30. Terry Eagleton, *The Illusions of Postmodernism* (Oxford: Blackwell, 1996), 28.

31. Augusto Del Noce, "Authority versus Power," *The Crisis of Modernity*, trans. Carlo Lancellotti, (Montreal: McGill-Queen's University Press, 2014), 236.

## Chapter Three

1. James Burnham, *Suicide of the West: An Essay on the Meaning and Destiny of Liberalism* (Regnery Books, Chicago: 1985), 201.

2. Burnham, *Suicide of the West*, 219.

3. Gianni Vattimo, *After Christianity*, Luca D'Isanto, trans. (New York: Columbia University Press, 2002), 55.

4. Vattimo, *After Christianity*, 68.

5. Ibid., 85.

6. Ibid., 77.

7. Ibid., 82.

8. Christopher Caldwell, *Reflections on the Revolution in Europe: Immigration, Islam, and the West* (Doubleday, New York: 2009), 330.

9. Vattimo, *After Christianity*, 113.

10. Burnham, *Suicide of the West*, 291.

## Chapter Four

1. Branko Milanovic, *Global Inequality: A New Approach for the Age of Globalization* (Cambridge, Mass.: Harvard University Press, 2016), 11.

2. Charles Duhigg and Keith Bradsher, "How the U.S. Lost Out on iPhone Work," *New York Times*, January 21, 2012.

3. David Farber, *The Rise and Fall of Modern Conservatism: A Short History* (Princeton, N.J.: Princeton University Press, 2010), 5.

4. Rachel Miletti, "Diversity Is Our Strength," Samuel Centre for Social Connectedness," https://www.socialconnectedness.org/diversity-is-our-strength/.

5. Peter Beinart, "The Racial and Religious Paranoia of Trump's Warsaw Speech," *The Atlantic*, July 6, 2017, https://www.theatlantic.com/international/archive/2017/07/trump-speech-poland/532866/.

## Chapter Five

1. Émile Durkheim, *The Elementary Forms of Religious Life*, Joseph Ward Swain, trans. (Mineola, N.Y.: Dover, 2008), 474.
2. Durkheim, *The Elementary Forms of Religious Life*, 475.
3. Ibid.
4. Ibid.
5. Ibid.
6. Ibid., 476.
7. Ibid.
8. Tony Blair, "Against Populism, the Center Must Hold," *New York Times*, May 3, 2017.

## Afterword

1. Jünger quoted in Nicolas Boyle, *Who Are We Now? Christian Humanism and the Global Market from Hegel to Heaney* (Edinburgh: T&T Clark, 1998), 215.
2. From Solzhenitsyn's speech "We Have Ceased to See the Purpose," delivered in 1993 at the International Academy of Philosophy in Liechtenstein; reprinted in Edward E. Ericson Jr. and Daniel J. Mahoney, eds., *The Solzhenitsyn Reader: New and Essential Writings, 1947–2005* (Wilmington, Del.: ISI Books, 2006), 591.

# Index

**A**

Acheson, Dean, 145–46
Adorno, Theodor, 16, 98
*Aeneid, The* (Virgil), 158
*After Christianity* (Vattimo), 78
Altizer, Thomas, 76
Arendt, Hannah, 142
Aristotle, 5, 34, 58, 141, 154–55
Auschwitz, x, xiv, xxv, 3, 8, 27, 70, 88, 89, 128, 130, 165
*Authoritarian Personality, The*, (Adorno et al.), 16, 18, 79, 93, 123

**B**

Baldwin, James, 161
Barth, Karl, 77
Barzun, Jacques, 36, 47
Becker, Gary, 37, 100
Beinart, Peter, 132
Blair, Tony, 142
Brexit, 123–24
Brown, Norman O., 45–47, 49, 69
Buckley, William F., Jr., 25–31, 74, 113

Bultmann, Rudolf, 77, 82
Burnham, James, 71–76, 94–95, 114
Bush, George H. W., 1–3, 31, 119, 133
Bush, George W., 62

**C**

Caldwell, Christopher, 85, 105
Camus, Albert, xxiii, 7, 52–57, 60–62, 76, 83, 89
capitalism, xxix, 11, 24, 49, 68, 107
*Capitalism and Freedom* (Friedman), 57, 60–61
Carter, Jimmy, 108
central planning, xxi, 20
*City of God, The* (Augustine), 150
*Civilization and Its Discontents* (Freud), 41–42
Clinton, Bill, 108, 119
Clinton, Hillary, 124
Cold War, 1, 72–75, 85, 109–10, 130, 145–46
Collectivism, 4, 20–22, 25–26, 130, 147
Conant, James B., 9–10, 33, 43

Cowen, Tyler, 37, 69
Cox, Harvey, 83–84

**D**
Dawkins, Richard, 55
Declaration of Independence, 26
Del Noce, Augusto, 68–69
Deneen, Patrick, xx
Deresiewicz, William, 104, 155
Derrida, Jacques, 64–69, 88, 92, 103,
    122–23

**E**
Eagleton, Terry, 69
Earned Income Tax Credit, 61
economic liberty, 24, 26, 30, 60, 108, 112
*Essays in the Public Philosophy*
    (Lippmann), 14–15, 118
European Union, 25, 108, 123, 127, 154

**F**
*Fall, The* (Camus), 54
fascism, xx, xxiv–xxv, xxvii–xxviii,
    11–13, 16, 18, 20–22, 27, 29, 52,
    105, 114, 125, 128, 130, 132, 142,
    145, 148
*Financial Times*, xxix
Fletcher, Joseph, 83
Foucault, Michel, 46–47
Frankfurt School, 16
French Revolution, xix, 136
Freud, Sigmund, 16, 40–42, 45, 49
Friedman, Milton, 56–63, 67–69,
    92–93, 108, 134, 147
Fromm, Erich, 5

**G**
Gehry, Frank, 99–100
*General Education in a Free Society*,
    33–36

Gilbert, Cass, 97
*God and Man at Yale* (Buckley),
    25–31, 113–14
great books, 34–36, 44, 66

**H**
Hamilton, William, 76
Hayek, Friedrich, 19–27, 29, 31, 38,
    48, 54, 56–57, 60, 63, 66–69, 75, 81,
    92–94, 101, 106, 109, 130, 134, 138,
    147–48, 150–52, 167
Heidegger, Martin, 86–91
Hittinger, Russell, 160
Hobbes, Thomas, 155–56
Hoffman, Abbie, 88
Honeyford, Ray, 126
Hussein, Saddam, 1
Hutchins, Robert Maynard, 44

**I**
immigration, 4, 94, 105, 125–27, 129,
    140, 142, 152, 156–57
individualism, 5, 11, 21–22, 24–27, 30,
    41, 161

**J**
Johnson, Philip, 99

**K**
Keynes, John Maynard, 26
Kohlberg, Lawrence, 13
Ku Klux Klan, xxvii–xxviii, 30

**L**
Le Corbusier, 98
Levinas, Emmanuel, 88
Lévy, Bernard-Henri, 67

liberalism, xv–xvi, xx, xxx, 10–11, 13–15, 21, 72–73, 94, 105, 107, 113, 141, 164–65
Libeskind, Daniel, 100
Lincoln, Abraham, 81
Lippmann, Walter, 14–15, 31, 73–74, 114, 118
Locke, John, xxix, 34, 155–56
London School of Economics, 19
*Lonely Crowd, The* (Riesman et al.), 43

**M**
MacIntyre, Alasdair, xx, 14
MacLeish, Archibald, 15
Madison, James, 58
Manhattan Project, 9
marriage, xxi, 37, 47, 51, 100, 104, 118, 121, 143, 149, 159, 160, 165
Marsden, George, 10
Marxism, 19–20, 67–68, 85
McGovern, George, 114
Merkel, Angela, 69, 127
Metz, Johann Baptist, 85
Middle East, 126
Milanovic, Branko, 109, 112
Mill, John Stuart, 22
Mont Pelerin Society, 19
Murray, Charles, 120
Murray, Douglas, 105, 126–27

**N**
National Socialism, 4, 20
Nazism, 2, 5, 19–20, 142, 153
*New Republic*, 15
*New Yorker*, xxix
*New York Times*, 111, 132
Newman, John Henry, 65

Nietzsche, 8, 10, 40, 64
Nixon, Richard, 115
nominalism, 6, 100, 164

**O**
Obama, Barack, 72, 117, 119–20, 122–23
Old Testament, 34, 80, 144, 159
*On Liberty* (Mill), 22
open borders, xi, 2–3, 31, 70, 125–27, 133, 147
*Open Society and Its Enemies, The* (Popper), 3, 8–9, 13, 19, 34, 39–40
Open Society Institute, 19
*Organization Man, The* (Whyte), 43
*Origins of Totalitarianism, The* (Arendt), 142

**P**
Paul, Darel, 124
Piketty, Thomas, 100
*Plague, The* (Camus), 52
Plato, 3–7, 10, 20, 34–35, 39–40, 67, 87, 89, 159
political correctness, x, xx, xxvi, 14, 18, 30, 47, 91, 105, 123, 131, 139, 152, 157, 165
Popper, Karl, 3–15, 18–23, 25, 29, 31, 34–35, 37–40, 45–48, 52, 63, 66–67, 74–75, 78, 81, 87, 89, 90–92, 94, 100–101, 106, 116, 130, 134, 138, 141, 147–48, 150–52, 158, 167
Powell, Lewis, 115
*Present at the Creation* (Acheson), 145
Providence College, 55

**R**
Rahner, Karl, 84–85
Rawls, John, 7, 59, 81, 89, 101

Reagan, Ronald, 108

Red Army, 132

Republican Party, 24, 29–30, 108, 114–15, 119, 125

Ricoeur, Paul, 40

Rieff, Philip, 168

Riesman, David, 43

*Road to Serfdom, The* (Hayek), 19–21, 24–26, 51

Robinson, John A. T., 76

Romney, Mitt, 119

Rorty, Richard, 80–81

**S**

Sartre, Jean-Paul, 7

Schlesinger, Arthur, Jr., 11–13, 18, 107, 112–13

Seymour, Charles, 27

Shapiro, Harold, 116

Silicon Valley, 69, 116

situation ethics, 83

Social Security, 61–62

Soros, George, 19

Southern Poverty Law Center, xxviii

Soviet Union, xix, 2, 9, 25, 108, 130

Spengler, Oswald, 90

*Suicide of the West* (Burnham), 71–72, 74–75, 94, 114

**T**

Taft, Robert, 113

Thoreau, Henry David, 58

Tillich, Paul, 93

totalitarianism, 5–6, 9, 11, 15–16, 19, 28–29, 40, 46, 48, 52, 55, 89, 93–94, 139

Trilling, Lionel, 36

Trump, Donald, xii–xiii, xx, xxviii–xxix, 112, 120, 124–25, 131–34, 140, 151

twentieth century, xvii, xix–xxi, xxiii–xxv, xxviii–xxix, 2, 7–8, 11–12, 14, 20, 31, 38, 55, 77, 82, 86, 97–98, 106, 108, 116, 136–37, 140, 143, 146, 158, 164–65

**U**

University of Chicago, 44

**V**

van Buren, Paul, 76

Vattimo, Gianni, 75–79, 81–83, 85–86, 88, 91–93, 101, 123, 139, 151

Vidal, Gore, 28

Vietnam, 75

**W**

Weaver, Richard, xxii, xxv

Weber, Max, 40, 66, 86, 90, 164

Western tradition, xx, xxv, 34–37, 39, 44–49, 80, 87, 118, 151

white supremacy, 125

Whyte, William, 43

William of Ockham, 6

Wood, Peter, 105

Woolworth, F. W., 97

World Trade Organization, 108

World War I, xi, xix, xxi, 2, 40, 90, 164

World War II, xxii, 1, 3, 10–12, 14, 16, 19–20, 29, 39, 45, 51, 72, 83–84, 98, 100, 132, 140, 142, 145–46, 161, 163

**X**

xenophobia, 35–36

**Y**

Yale Review, 15

Yale University, 25–28, 30, 74